GW00870683

The Island of Poe

To Stewart

Long time through life, — means that things do last — Poe has lasted me over 40 years.

Enjoy the beauty in the writing Spread the Word

Gerry Parkin

The Island of Poe
Tony Parkin

Slippery Jacks Press

The Island of Poe

Copyright © Tony Parkin 2009

All Rights Reserved

No part of this book may be reproduced in any form
by photocopying or by any electronic or mechanical means,
including information storage and retrieval systems,
without permission in writing from both the copyright
owner and the publisher of this book.

ISBN 978-0-9556200-8-9

This book is a faithful representation of Tony Parkin's stage show.

Cover art by Ben Farquharson

First published 2009 by Slippery Jacks Press
Printed for Slippery Jacks
www.slipperyjacks.com

Dedicated to Edgar and Virgina Poe
and Maria Clemm

With grateful acknowledgement to
Edgar Allan Poe

The Raven, Lenore, Hymn, A Valentine, The
Coliseum, To Helen, Alone, To_____Bridal Ballad
To F_____Al Aaraaf, Sonnet to Science
To the River, Tamerlane, To___, A Dream,
Romance, Fairy-Land, The Lake__To___ Song
To Mary Louise Shew, To_____Ulalume, The Bells
An Enigma, Annabel Lee, To my Mother, The
Haunted Palace, The Conqueror Worm, To
Frances Sargent Osgood, To One in Paradise,
The Valley of Unrest, The City Beneath the Sea,
Silence, The Sleeper, A Dream Within A Dream,
Dream-Land, Eulalie, To Zante, Eldorado, Israfel,
For Annie, Scenes from Politian (A Tragedy)
Eureka (A Prose Poem)

The Adventures of Hans Pfaall, The Gold Bug, The Balloon-Hoax, Von Kempelen & His Discovery, Mesmeric Revelation. The Facts in the Case of Msr Valdemar, MS Found in a Bottle, 1.0002, Tale of Scheherazade, Descent into the Maelstrom, Murders in the Rue Morgue, Mystery of Marie Roget, The Purloined Letter, The Black Cat, The Fall of the House of Usher, Berenice, The Pit and the Pendulum. The Premature Burial, The Oval Portrait, The Masque of the Red Death, The Cask of Amontillado, The Imp of the Perverse, The Island of Fay, The Assignation, The Tell-Tale Heart, The Domain of Arnheiin, Landor's Cottage, Narrative of Arthur Gordon Pym, William Wilson, Eleonora, Ligeia, Morella, Metzengerstein, Angel of the Odd, A Predicament, The System of Dr Tarr & Professor Fether, Xing a Paragrab, Mystification The Literary Life of Thingum Bob, Diddling as an Exact Science,. How to Write a Blackwood Article, Mellonta Tauta, The Business Man, The Man that was Used Up, Loss of Breath, The Spectacles, The Landscape Garden, Maelzel's Chess Player, Lionizing, Philosophy of Furniture,

A Tale of Jerusalem, Shadow, Silence,
Tale of the Ragged Mountains. The Duc de
L'omelette, The Oblong Box, King Pest, Three
Sundays in a week, Why the Little Frenchman wears
his arm in a sling, Bon-Bon, The Devil in the Belfry,
Man of the Crowd, The Sphinx,
The Homo-cameleopard, Toby Dammit, Hop-Frog.

Review of Stephen's Arabia Petraea, Letter to B------
Magazine Writing, Peter Snook, The Quacks of
Helicon, Astoria, The Poetic Principle, Rationale of
Verse Philosophy of Composition, Power of Words,
George Bush.

Colloquy of Monos and Una, N.P. Willis,
Conversation between Eiros & Charmion, William
Kirkland of Criticism Public & Private, George H.
Colton William M. Gillespie, Chas. F. Briggs, Ralph
Hoytt, John W. Francis, Anna Cora Mowatt,
Charles Anthon, George B. Cheever, Gulian C.
Verplanck Sarah Marg.

Freeman Hunt, Piero Maroncelli, Laughton Osborn,
Fitz-Greene Halleck, Ann S. Stephens, Evert A.
Duyckinck, Mary Gove Nichols, James Aldrich,
Henry Carey, Chris. Pease Cranch, James Lawson,
Caroline M. Kirkland, Epes Sargent, Frances
Sargent Osgood, Prosper M. Watmore, Lydia M.
Child, Emma C. Embury , Thomas Dunn Brown,
Elizabeth Bogart, Anne C. Lynch, Catherine M.
Sedgwick, Lewis Gaylord Clark, Mary E. Hewitt,
Charles Fenno Hoffman, Richard Adam Locke,

Rufus Dawes, Elizabeth Oakes Smith, J.G.C. Barnard, William W. Lord, Thomas Ward "Platlus", William Cullen Bryant, Seba Smith, Nathaniel Hawthorne, Elizabeth Frieze Ellett, Bayard Taylor, Margaret Miller & Lucretia Mara Davidson, William Ellery, Channing, William Ross Wallack, Estelle Anne Lewis, Joel T. Headley, George P. Morris, Robert M. Bird, Cornelius Matthews, William Gilmore Simms, Rufus W. Griswold, James Russell Lowell, Mr Longfellow & Other Plagiarists, Longfellow, Willis, American Drama, Thomas More, Longfellow's Ballads, Rodman Drake, Fancy & Imagination, E.P. Whipple, & Other Critics, J. Fenimore Copper, Elizabeth Barrett Barrett, R.H. Horne, Thomas Babington Macaulay, Charles Lever, Francis Maryat, Henry Cockton, Charles Dickens, Fifty Suggestions.

A Poem dedicated to Edgar Allan Poe

The Valley, the Dell,
The knell of the bell.
The Tell-Tale Heart
The Heaven, the Hell,
The Pit, the Pendulum,
The wheel, the well,
The Taglay Mist
That daily fell
Upon my head,
Who saw the dread?
The dread; I knew?
Did they misconstrue?
Was it true? Was it true?
Did I discover
O constant lover!
A Time and Tide
Of my very own
The beyond of Life
Beyond the grave,
Did I travel?

A Poem dedicated to Edgar Allan Poe

He, whose mind is free
Of these earthly chains
That pin him down,
Lifeless — he yields
To its rigid automaton
And becomes a cog.

In the universal clock
Of the world, to tick
And tick, in time
With time, to tick in Time
It took a man
Of mind as mine,
To show the way
Others can find.
The journey that
Exists within
The skull, the cranium
The brain, the skin.
Manipulate your
Spirit hence
Feast on life's
Exuberance.
Receive the wine

A Poem dedicated to Edgar Allan Poe

And let it flow
Pathed with feeling all aglow
You will then discover,
O constant lover!
Life, is the art
We must all discover.

Tony Parkin copyright 1971

Chapter One – Edgar the Legitimate

"No man is an Island unto himself'" – Quote!

However, one feels that Edgar Allan Poe <u>was</u> an island. Few people reached his heights, few were found on his beach, maybe a few pebbles, of disenchanted writers; for Poe was a master of his generation; and his cup overflowed.

'How I laboured, how I toiled, how I wrote, Ye Gods, did I not write...I knew not the word 'ease'... The Style! That was the Thing!

Poe was prolific, in the extreme; between his bouts of drunken alcoholism and illnesses. His Mother was a travelling actress, but, was resident in Boston, Mass. when Poe was born.

She toured with what is now known as 'Summer Stock', in England it would be called Repertory. Poe was fed 'gin-sops!' as she suffered from TB and could not give breast milk. This was cotton wool, dipped in 'Mother's Ruin' the Gin-Bottle!

Chapter One – Edgar the Legitimate
`

Poe's mother was 21, but, she had also been married before. It was not unusual in those days for girls to be married at fourteen. Life expectancy was 'lucky to get beyond forty,' as there were <u>no</u> cures for any illnesses. Poe actually married his cousin Virginia when he was 27, and she was only 13. It was a 'marriage of convenience,' so he could have his 'Muddy' -Auntie Maria Clemm to act as his 'real' mother, and he had a ready-made family, (for Virginia was no more than a child) -without consummation!

However, Poe's first introduction to life was travelling with his mother to Richmond, Charleston and Norfolk, after his real father did a disappearing act. He had taken to drink, and perhaps the drink had taken to him, no one knows how he died! However, the sins of the father were to be visited on America's 'Favourite' son.

This is what Poe should have been, but he chose an 'enemy' whom he thought was a friend, to publish his Works. Consequently, Poe needs to be seen as a human being, who was only 'an Island' because he was a Genius!

Chapter One – Edgar the Legitimate

His first appearance on stage was as a bulge in Cordelia's belly, while his father played Edmund in King Lear. So, Poe received his name from 'The Bard,' as 'Edgar the legitimate' son of the Duke of Gloucester. David Poe, his Father, had distinctive relatives in England and Scotland, the Poe's and the Galt's which would have an influence over the young aspiring Poet/Writer, and at that time, he would also benefit financially.

"My Uncle William Galt died in 1824, - leaving enough money for a completely new house, I was given a private tutor, and sent to the University of Virginia.

….A pleasant home, fine clothes to wear, slaves to dress me …
….I had reached the pinnacle of my 'comfortable' Youth."

Poe's 'gait' therefore was handed down on his father's side and his 'stage' voice came in useful when reciting at School, and University, to fellow-students, and later in life when he was Lecturing.

Chapter One – Edgar the Legitimate
`

He had a resonant voice, and won First Prize for elocution at school (due to his English training). When he was thirteen, Joseph Clarke, his Schoolmaster, found an Anthology of his Poetry, while marking his arithmetic. He was noted for his swimming, too, from Ludlams Wharf to Warwick on the James' River. Quite a feat for a young boy.

Poe was adopted by a Mr. Allan when he was three. Mr. Allan ran a general store under the name of Ellis and Allan. Poe lived with his new step-mother, but Mr. Allan had many off-spring from various infidelities. They would receive monies which would have helped Poe, - especially when he needed it, most. Worst of all, Poe was in dire need when Mr. Allan died in 1834; leaving nothing in his will, to his adopted 'Genius'.

"When I attribute to myself the name of 'Genius', there is no doubt in my mind, ponder awhile upon my works, and you will see that 'even in the grave, all is not lost'. The imagination and veracity of my mind reached beyond the grave, and grasped a world which is out of reach of ye ordinary mortals."

`

A land where Man and his Soul are Eternal, where all is visual, dramatic and full of the essence of Art and Poetry. A Creation of a Creation. Where Shadow is Substance, and Substance is Being, and Being is Imagination. Imagination is Being. The Dreamer, dreams, the Dreamer lives, - lives within his dream. He builds the wall around himself and becomes a prisoner of the mind.

A prisoner in his own World, yet this is the Fantasy World, the one he believes in, yours is the Physical world, the one he disbelieves, there he is a Prisoner by God's Making. Here, in his own world, it is his own being, his own cell. A Cell of Despair, of fear, without a glimmering of hope, for he no longer wishes nor wills himself to wake; not because he fears dreaded objects all around, but that he fears there may be nothing to see. Then, as the Prisoner of the Mind and the Prisoner of Life begin to face the world, there is one essence equal in both the physical and the spiritual person, and that is DOUBT!"

Chapter One – Edgar the Legitimate

During the whole of a dull, dark, and soundless day in the autumn of the year, when the clouds hung oppressively low in the heavens, I had been passing alone, on horseback, through a singularly dreary tract of country; and at length found myself, as the shades of the evening drew on, within view of the melancholy House of Usher.

I know not how it was - but, with the first glimpse of the building, a sense of insufferable gloom pervaded my spirit. I say insufferable; for the feeling was unrelieved by any of that half-pleasurable, because poetic, sentiment with which the mind usually receives even the sternest natural images of the desolate or terrible. I looked upon the scene before me, - upon the mere house, and the simple landscape features of the domain, upon the bleak walls, upon the vacant eye-like windows, upon a few rank sedges, and upon a few white trunks of decayed trees, - with an utter depression of soul which I can compare to no other earthly sensation more properly than to the after-dream of the reveller upon opium: the bitter lapse into everyday life, the hideous dropping off of the veil.

Chapter One – Edgar the Legitimate

"I had swooned, but still will not say that all of consciousness was lost. In the deepest slumber, - no! In delirium, - no! In a swoon, - no. In death, - no! Even in the grave, all is not lost! Arousing from the most profound of slumbers we break the gossamer web of some dream."

Chapter Two – I wrapp'd myself in grandeur, then...

People, have said of my verse, it is lyrical and melancholy, and described as Spiritual, - that is certain for it did not spring from the Earth, but grew out of the turmoil of my mind.... You shall Judge.

Tamerlane

Kind solace in a dying hour!
Such, father, is not (now) my theme
I will not madly deem that power
Of Earth may shrive me of the sin
Unearthly pride hath revell'd in -
I have no time to dote or dream!
You call it hope - that fire of fire!
It is but agony of desire:
If I can hope - O God! I can -
Its fount is holier - more divine -
I would not call thee fool, old man,
But such is not a gift of thine.

Chapter Two – I wrapp'd myself in grandeur, then...

Know thou the secret of a spirit
Bowed from its wild pride into shame,
O yearning heart! I did inherit
Thy withering portion with the fame,
The searing glory which hath shone
Amid the jewels of my throne,
Halo of Hell! and with a pain
Not Hell shall make me fear again -
O craving heart! for the lost flowers
And sunshine of my summer hours!
The undying voice of that dead time,
With its interminable chime,
Rings, in the spirit of a spell,
Upon thy emptiness - a knell.

I have not always been as now:
The fevered diadem on my brow
I claimed and won usurpingly -
Hath not the same fierce heirdom given
Rome to Caesar - this to me?
The heritage of a kingly mind,
And a proud spirit which hath striven
Triumphantly with human kind.

Chapter Two – I wrapp'd myself in grandeur, then...

On mountain soil I first drew life:
The mists of the Taglay have shed
Nightly their dews upon my head,
And I believe, the winged strife
And tumult of the headlong air
Have nestled in my very hair.

The rain came down upon my head
Unshelter'd - and the heavy wind
Rendered me mad and deaf and blind.
It was but man, I thought, who shed
Laurels upon me: and the rush -
The torrent of the chilly air
Gurgled within my ear - the crush
Of empires - with the captive's prayer -
The hum of suitors - and the tone
Of flattery 'round a sovereign's throne.

My passions, from that hapless hour,
Usurped a tyranny which men
Have deemed since I have reached to power
My innate nature - be it so;
But, father, there lived one who, then,

Chapter Two – I wrapp'd myself in grandeur, then...

Then - in my boyhood - when their fire
Burn'd with a still intenser glow
(For passion must, with youth, expire)
E'en then who knew this iron heart
In woman's weakness had a part.

There were three women that were prominent in Poe's teenage years. He was a very introverted boy and used to wander home alone to his beloved step-mother. Then, he was introduced to Robert Stanard and met his mother: Jan 'Helen' Stith Stanard - Poe was entranced by her:

"She lived in a stately home, with every luxury off-setting her own beauty; she became my Helen!"

When she died, of consumption and madness (a fate of the period), he was only fifteen, and spent many hours by her grave (unusual in one so young).

To Helen

Helen, thy beauty is to me
Like those Nicéan barks of yore.
That gently o'er a perfumed sea
The weary, wayworn wanderer bore
To his own native shore.

On desperate seas long wont to roam,
Thy hyacinth hair, thy classic face,
Thy Naiad airs have brought me home
To the glory that was Greece
And the grandeur that was Rome.

Lo! in yon brilliant window niche
How statue-like I see thee stand,
The agate lamp within thy hand!
Ah, Psyche, from the regions which
Are Holy Land!

Chapter Two – I wrapp'd myself in grandeur, then...

"Lieutenant Poe, was my new title, - when I joined the Junior Morgan Riflemen. While revelling in this new-found glory, the gaze of all females: yet still pursuing my melancholy at Helen's grave; Father's business grew worse. He began to go out of business and during the next few years he wound up his affairs. My Foster-Father took a disgruntled view to my poetry and my gadding about; he did not understand that I was not ungrateful; merely taking advantage of the effects God had given me, while still young and able to enjoy them.

It was during my sixteenth year that I fell in love with Sarah Elmira Royster. We were both in love with love, I drew her portrait, but rather than flatter her with my own poems I quoted her the wit of Byron."

O, she was worthy of all love!
Love - as infancy - was mine -
'Twas such an angel minds above
Might envy: her young heart the shrine
On which my every hope and thought
Were incense - then a goodly gift

Chapter Two – I wrapp'd myself in grandeur, then...

For they were childish and upright -
Pure as her young example taught;
Why did I leave it, and adrift,
Trust to the fire within for light?

We grew in age - and love - together -
Roaming the forest, and the wild;
My breast her shield in wintry weather -
And, when the friendly sunshine smiled.
And she would mark the opening skies,
I saw no heaven - but in her eyes.
Young Love's first lesson is - the heart;
For 'mid that sunshine and those smiles,
When, from our little cares apart,
And laughing at her girlish wiles,
I'd throw me on her throbbing breast,
And pour my spirit out in tears -
There was no need to speak the rest –
No need to quiet any fears
Of her - who ask'd no reason why,
But turn'd on me her quiet eye!

Chapter Two – I wrapp'd myself in grandeur, then...

I spoke to her of power and pride,
But mystically - in such guise
That she might deem it nought beside
The moment's converse: in her eyes
I read, perhaps too carelessly-
A mingled feeling with my own -
The flush on her bright cheek, to me
Seem'd to become a queenly throne
Too well that I should let it be
Light in the wilderness alone.

I wrapp'd myself in grandeur then,
And donn'd a visionary crown -
Yet it was not that Fantasy
Had thrown her mantle over me -
But, that among the rabble - men,
Lion Ambition is chained down -
And crouches to a keeper's hand -
Not so in deserts where the grand -
The wild - the terrible conspire
With their own breath to fan his fire.

Chapter Two – I wrapp'd myself in grandeur, then...

Look 'round thee now on Samarcand!-
Is she not Queen of Earth? her pride
Above all cities? in her hand
Their destinies? in all beside
Of glory which the world hath known
Stands she not nobly and alone?
Falling - her veriest stepping - stone
Shall form the pedestal of a throne -
And who her sovereign? Timour - he
Whom the astonished people saw
Striding o'er empires haughtily
A diadem'd outlaw.

O human love! thou spirit given,
On Earth, of all we hope in Heaven.
Which fall'st into the soul like rain
Upon the Siroc - withered plain,
And, failing in thy power to bless,
But leav'st the heart a wilderness!
Idea! which bindest life around
With music of so strange a sound
And beauty of so wild a birth -
Farewell! for I have won the Earth.

Chapter Two — I wrapp'd myself in grandeur, then...

"Thus, at seventeen, I had everything, - myself a smart, young, Virginian gentleman, with an excellent schooling background, a pleasant home, fine clothes to wear, slaves to dress me, and engaged to a beautiful girl who was an ideal to Truth and Beauty. All set to start the last stage of my Literary education at the University. I had reached the pinnacle of my Comfortable Youth."

Alas, for Poe <u>that</u> was the <u>pinnacle</u> - where he would feel secure!!' It was the end of what started as an insecure birth to an ideal childhood of some fourteen years. Well educated, - a Poet, - top in several subjects, adept at sports, and carrying himself with impeccable taste and sobriety (note) and respect for his dress and accent!! Poe was a most eligible bachelor!

The happiest day - the happiest hour
My seared and blighted heart hath known
The highest hope of pride and power
I feel hath flown.
Of power. said I? Yes. such I ween
But they have vanished long, alas!'
The visions of my Youth have been - -
But let them pass.

Chapter Two – I wrapp'd myself in grandeur, then...

And pride, what have I now with thee?
Another brow may e'en inherit
The venom thou hast poured on me -
Be still my spirit!

The happiest day - the happiest hour
Mine eyes shall see - have ever seen
The brightest glance of pride and power
I feel have been
But were that hope of pride and power
Now offered with the pain
Ev'n then I felt - that brightest hour
I would not live again.

Alas, when Poe was at University, his letters were
intercepted by her father, Mr Royster, who
confiscated them (think: what they would be worth,
today!!')

So, poor Elmira and poor Poe, they would not meet
again until he saw her with her husband, and then, later,
when she was Mrs Shelton, a widow, and he was in the
last year of his life. They arranged to marry, were
betrothed, - but never made the match.

Chapter Two – I wrapp'd myself in grandeur, then...

Her three brothers were against it, and Poe felt he
was followed, - and may have even been 'roughed-up' by
them. This is mere surmise. The widow, Mrs Shelton
warmed to Poe, he had done nothing wrong in her eyes,
and she remembered when they gambolled in the fields
. . .

I'd throw me on her throbbing breast,
And pour my spirit out in tears ....

Poe described the "beauty" of life through his poetry.
But also showed how he would liked to have lived his own
Life - but could not. He chose to live in "Dreams."

Oh! that my young life were a lasting dream!
My spirit not awakening, till the beam
Of an eternity should bring the morrow.
Yes, tho' that long dream were of hopeless sorrow,
'Twere better than a cold reality
Of waking life, to him whose heart must be,
And hath been still, upon the lovely earth,
A chaos of deep passion, from his birth.
But should it be - that dream eternally

Chapter Two – I wrapp'd myself in grandeur, then...

Continuing - as dreams have been to me
In my young boyhood - should it thus be given
'Twere folly still to hope for higher Heaven.
For I have revell'd, when the sun was bright
I' the summer sky, in dreams of living light
And loveliness, - have left my very heart
In climes of my imagining, apart,
From mine own home, with beings that have been
Of mine own thought - what more could I have seen?
'Twas once - and once only - and the wild hour
From my remembrance shall not pass - some power
Or spell had bound me - 'twas the chilly wind
Came o'er me in the night, and left behind
Its image on my spirit - or the moon,
Shone on my slumbers in her lofty noon,
Too coldly - or the stars - howe'er it was
That dream was as that night-wind - let it pass.
I have been happy, - tho' in a dream.
I have been happy - and I love the theme:
Dreams! in their vivid colouring of life,
As in that fleeting, shadowy, misty strife
Of semblance with reality, which brings
To the delirious eye, more lovely things

Chapter Two – I wrapp'd myself in grandeur, then...

Of paradise and love - and all our own!
Than young hope in his sunniest hour bath known.

When hope, that eagle that tower'd, could see
No cliff beyond him in the sky
His pinions were bent droopingly -
And homeward turn'd his softened eye.
'Twas sunset: when the sun will part
There comes a sullenness of heart
To him who still would look upon
The glory of the summer sun.
That soul will hate the ev'ning mist
So often lovely, and will list
To the sound of the coming darkness (known
to those whose spirits hearken) as one
Who, in a dream of night, would fly
But cannot, from a danger nigh.

What tho' the moon - the white moon
Shed all the splendour of her noon,
Her smile is chilly - and her beam,
In that time of dreariness, will seem
(So like you gather in your breath)

Chapter Two – I wrapp'd myself in grandeur, then...

A portrait taken after death.
And boyhood is a summer sun
Whose waning is the dreariest one -
For all we live to know is known
And all we seek to keep bath flown -
Let life, then, as the day-flower, fall
With the noon-day beauty - which is all.

I do believe that Eblis hath
A snare in every human path -
Else how, when in the holy grove
I wandered of the idol, love, -
Who daily scents his snowy wings
With incense of burnt offerings
From the most unpolluted things
Whose pleasant bowers are yet so riven
Above with trellis'd rays from Heaven
No mote may shun -no tiniest fly -
The lightning of his eagle eye -
How was it that Ambition crept,
Unseen amid the revels there,
Till growing bold, he laughed and leapt
In the tangles of Love's very hair?

Chapter Two – I wrapp'd myself in grandeur, then...

Poe chose Ambition, - his writing rather than love, - relationships; and close friends. It was a <u>mistake</u> for Poe <u>needed</u> Love and Friendship - more than anyone, and it was sadly lacking at great moments in his Life!!

However; the gift that Poe gave to the world was 'unsurpassable' because what Poe created in his life was something that had rarely been touched before in writing. His futuristic outlook, and Predictions would inspire and influence authors for the next hundred and fifty years. The films of his stories, (though, quite 'tongue in cheek', nevertheless did help towards his fame; thanks much to Roger Corman, Vincent Price, and

Peter Lorre: Among these were 'House of Usher', 'The Pit and The Pendulum', 'The Premature Burial' (Starring Ray Milland), 'Tales of Terror' (which included 'Morella'), 'The Black Cat' (incorporating 'The Cask of Amontillado'), and 'The Facts in the Case of Monsieur Valdemar' (where Vincent Price dissolves into Putridity). 'The Haunted Palace', 'The Masque of the Red Death' (Incorporating 'Hop-Frog'), 'The Tomb of Ligeia', and 'The Raven'.

This was his most famous work, and it gained him his own newspaper! The Raven became the name that he was known by, and he tells how he wrote it in his Philosophy of Composition.

Chapter Three – The Search for the Soul

During this period he corresponded with Charles Dickens and even predicted the 'end' of 'Barnaby Rudge' after he sent him a draft of his first chapter. 'The Gold Bug' and 'Murders in the Rue Morgue' found him fame in France, and thanks to Baudelaire that fame lasted so he was more popular in Europe than England, until early 20th Century. Debussy also wrote an opera to him, basing it on 'Usher'.

The reason that Poe was not well-recognised, at first, was due to Rufus W. Griswold, his phlegmatic publisher, to whom he entrusted his entire works. Rufus W. Griswold maligned Poe behind his back and when Poe was dead. No one remembers anything that Griswold wrote, - he only received fame as Poe's publisher, Griswold could not touch Poe, - but he made sure Poe was unknown in England until Elmira and Sarah Helen Whitman broke their silence, and J.H. Ingram (An Englishman) started gathering the Works together. Griswold was the worst person Poe could have chosen, as they both aspired to the love of Sarah Helen Whitman, - and Griswold ensured she knew of Poe's drunkenness, and he may have been responsible for the story about Edgar's `early morning nips' during his time on the Southern Literary Messenger.

So, their engagement was `nipped in the bud', despite the preparations made with Mrs Whitman's mother and Maria Clemm. However, the roles were soon reversed as Poe influenced so many writers and gained his own notoriety and everlasting fame, while Griswold sank into oblivion. Even Conan Doyle recognised Poe as his inspiration for Sherlock Holmes from the analytical detective Msr C. Auguste Dupin who appears in Poe's stories: The Purloined Letter; The Murders in the Rue Morgue; and The Mystery of Marie Roget (this, was based on a true story, reported in the newspapers of the time). Poe gained his first editorship, just after his grandmother died.

`1835. Grandma Poe died and her pension with her. I, being the only beneficiary, became editor of the Southern Literary Messenger at the age of 26.

Chapter Three – The Search for the Soul

I was now accepted to a social system, where only success
counted, failure was unheard of and descried. This led
to drunken debauches and occasionally I would find myself
in bed, not knowing how I had reached my repose. I was
affluent and in circulation, receiving the begging letters,
instead of sending them, but, the drink had its effect
and even a nip in the morning was required to restore my
senses.

After a trial month I rushed to Baltimore to collect my
cousin and Auntie Maria. We resided in a boarding-
house; and my prolific output paid more than my basic
salary, but I was sworn to remain sober.

As the circulation increased my own contributions
slackened off, and I turned to my cousin Virginia. Our
marriage was imminent, though Virginia was only 13,
and I was 27.

I reviewed Daniel Defoe's Robinson Crusoe; which
inspired The Adventures of Arthur Gordon Pym,
and left the Messenger in 1837".

Chapter Three – The Search for the Soul

"A city of narrow streets, mud-tracks, fit only for horse and cart, this was New York, where I went to write for the Review. I charmed a bookseller, William Gowans, to become our lodger. He was naturally affected by Virginia's beauty and Mrs Clemm's housekeeping. The country was going through an economic crisis and The Review was suspended. We moved to 113½ Carmine Street, and it was the lodgers that paid enough to keep me at my manuscripts. Arthur Gordon Pym was penned, but, I had failed to conquer New York. It afforded a move to Philadelphia, a city struggling for supremacy over New York. 1838, Philadelphia, and the search for the soul!"

Eulalie

I dwelt alone
In a world of moan,
And my soul was a stagnant tide,
Till the fair and gentle Eulalie became my blushing bride
-
Till the yellow-haired young Eulalie became my smiling
bride.

Now doubt - now pain
Come never again,
For her soul gives me sigh for sigh,
And all day long
Shines, bright and strong,
Astarte within the sky
While ever to her dear Eulalie upturns
her matron eye -
While ever to her young Eulalie upturns
her violet eye.

Chapter Four – I heard many things in hell

My stories have been called frightening and macabre, it is for you to say "Nay!"

The Tell-Tale Heart

True! - nervous - very, very dreadfully nervous I had been and am; but why will you say that I am mad? The disease had sharpened my senses - not destroyed - not dulled them. Above all was the sense of hearing acute. I heard all things in the heaven and in the earth. I heard many things in hell. How, then, am I mad? Hearken! and observe how healthily - how calmly I can tell you the whole story.

It is impossible to say how first the idea entered my brain: but once conceived, it haunted me day and night. Object there was none. Passion there was none. I loved the old man. He had never wronged me. He had never given me insult. For his gold I had no desire. I think it was his eye! yes, it was this! He had the eye of a vulture - a pale blue eye, with a film over it.

Chapter Four – I heard many things in hell

Whenever it fell upon me, my blood ran cold: and so by degrees - very gradually - I made up my mind to take the life of the old man, and thus rid myself of the eye forever.

Now this is the point. You fancy me mad. Madmen know nothing. But you should have seen me. You should have seen how wisely I proceeded - with what caution - with what foresight - with what dissimulation I went to work! I was never kinder to the old man than during the whole week before I killed him. And every night, about midnight, I turned the latch of his door and opened it - oh so gently! And then, when I had made an opening sufficient for my head, I put in a dark lantern, all closed, closed, so that no light shone out, and then I thrust in my head. Oh, you would have laughed to see how cunningly I thrust it in!

I moved it slowly - very, very slowly, so that I might not disturb the old man's sleep. It took me an hour to place my whole head within the opening so far that I could see him as he lay upon his bed. Ha! would a madman have been so wise as this? And then, when my head was well in the room, I undid the lantern cautiously -oh so

Chapter Four – I heard many things in hell

cautiously - cautiously (for the hinges creaked) - I undid
it just so much that a single thin ray fell upon the vulture
eye. And this I did for seven long nights -every night
just at midnight - but I found the eye always closed; and
so it was impossible to do the work; for it was not the old
man who vexed me, but his Evil Eye. And every
morning, when the day broke, I went boldly into the
chamber, and spoke courageously to him, calling him by
name in a hearty tone, and inquiring how he had passed
the night. So you see he would have been a very
profound old man, indeed, to suspect that every night,
just at twelve, I looked in upon him while he slept.

Upon the eighth night I was more than usually cautious
in opening the door. A watch's minute hand moves more
quickly than did mine. Never before that night, had I
felt the extent of my own powers - of my sagacity. I
could scarcely contain my feelings of triumph. To think
that there I was, opening the door, little by little, and he
not even to dream of my secret deeds or thoughts. I
fairly chuckled at the idea; and perhaps he heard me;
for he moved on the bed suddenly, as if startled. Now
you may think that I drew back - but no. his room was as
black as pitch with the thick darkness (for the shutters

Chapter Four – I heard many things in hell

were close fastened, through fear of robbers), and so I
knew that he could not see the opening of the door, and
I kept pushing it on steadily, steadily.

I had my head in, and was about to open the lantern,
when my thumb slipped upon the tin fastening, and the
old man sprang up in bed, crying out "Who's there?"
I kept quite still and said nothing. For a whole hour I
did not move a muscle, and in the meantime I did not
hear him lie down. He was still sitting up in the bed
listening; - just as I have done, night after night,
hearkening to the death watches in the wall.

Presently I heard a slight groan, and I knew it was a
groan of mortal terror. It was not a groan of pain or of
grief - oh, no!' - it was the low stifled sound that arises
from the bottom of the soul when overcharged with awe.
I knew the sound well. Many a night, just at midnight,
when all the world slept, it has welled up from my own
bosom, deepening, with its dreadful echo, the terrors
that distracted me. I say I knew it well. I knew what the
old man felt, and pitied him, although I chuckled at
heart. I knew that he had been lying awake ever since
the first slight noise, when he had turned in the bed.

Chapter Four – I heard many things in hell

His fears had been ever since growing upon him. He
had been trying to fancy them causeless, but could not.
He had been saying to himself - "It is nothing but the
wind in the chimney - it is only a mouse crossing the
floor," or "it is merely a cricket which has made a single
chirp." Yes, he had been trying to comfort himself with
these suppositions: but he had found all in vain. All in
vain; because Death, in approaching him had stalked
with his black shadow before him, and enveloped the
victim. And it was the mournful influence of the
unperceived shadow that caused him to feel - although he
neither saw nor heard - to feel the presence of my head
within the room.

When I had waited a long time, very patiently, without
hearing him lie down, I resolved to open a little - a very,
very little crevice in the lantern. So I opened it - you
cannot imagine how stealthily, stealthily - until, at length
a single dim ray, like the thread of a spider, shot from
out the crevice and fell full upon the vulture eye.
It was open-wide, wide open - and I grew furious as I
gazed upon it. I saw it with a perfect distinctness - all a
dull blue, with a hideous veil over it that chilled the very
marrow in my bones; but I could see nothing else of the

Chapter Four – I heard many things in hell

old man's face or person: for I had directed the ray, as
if by instinct, precisely upon the damned spot.

And have I not told you that what you mistake for
madness is but over acuteness of the senses? - now, I
say, there came to my ears a low, dull, quick sound, such
as a watch makes when enveloped in cotton. I knew that
sound well, too. It was the beating of the old man's
heart. It increased my fury, as the beating of a drum
stimulates the soldier into courage.

But even yet I refrained and kept still. I scarcely
breathed. I held the lantern motionless. I tried how
steadily I could maintain the ray upon the eye.
Meantime the hellish tattoo of the heart increased. It
grew quicker and quicker, louder and louder every
instant. The old man's terror must have been extreme!
It grew louder, I say, louder every moment! - do you
mark me well?

Chapter Four – I heard many things in hell

I have told you that I am nervous: so I am. And now at the dead hour of the night, amid the dreadful silence of that old house, so strange a noise as this excited me to uncontrollable terror. Yet, for some minutes longer I refrained and stood still. But the beating grew louder, louder! I thought the heart must burst. And now a new anxiety seized me - the sound would be heard by a neighbour! The old man's hour had come! With a loud yell, I threw open the lantern and leaped into the room. He shrieked once - once only. In an instant I dragged him to the floor, and pulled the heavy bed over him. I then smiled gaily, to find the deed so far done. But, for many minutes, the heart beat on with a muffled sound. This, however, did not vex me; it would not be heard through the wall. At length it ceased. The old man was dead. I removed the bed and examined the corpse. Yes, he was stone, stone dead. I placed my hand upon the heart and held it there many minutes. There was no pulsation. He was stone dead. His eye would trouble me no more.

Chapter Four – I heard many things in hell

If still you think me mad, you will think so no longer when
I describe the wise precautions I took for the
concealment of the body. The night waned, and I
worked hastily, but in silence. First of all I dismembered
the corpse. I cut off the head and the arms and the
legs.

I then took up three planks from the flooring of the
chamber, and deposited all between the scantlings. I then
replaced the boards so cleverly, so cunningly, that no
human eye - not even his - could have detected anything
wrong. There was nothing to wash out - no stain of any
kind - no blood-spot whatever. I had been too wary for
that. A tub had caught all -ha ha!

When I had made an end of these labours, it was four
o'clock -still dark as midnight. As the bell sounded the
hour, there came a knocking at the street door. I went
down to open it with a light heart, - for what had I now
to fear? There entered three men, who introduced
themselves, with perfect suavity, as officers of the
police. A shriek had been heard by a neighbour during
the night; suspicion of foul play had been aroused;
information had been lodged at the police office, and

Chapter Four – I heard many things in hell

they (the officers) had been deputed to search the premises.

I smiled, - for what had I to fear? I bade the gentlemen welcome. The shriek, I said, was my own in a dream. The old man, I mentioned, was absent in the country. I took my visitors all over the house. I bade them search - search well. I led them, at length, to his chamber. I showed them his treasures, secure, undisturbed. In the enthusiasm of my confidence, I brought chairs into the room, and desired them here to rest from their fatigues, while I myself, in the wild audacity of my perfect triumph, placed my own seat upon the very spot beneath which reposed the corpse of the victim.

The officers were satisfied. My manner had convinced them. I was singularly at ease. They sat, and while I answered cheerily, they chatted of familiar things. But, ere long, I felt myself getting pale and wished them gone. My head ached and I fancied a ringing in my ears: but still they sat and still chatted.

Chapter Four – I heard many things in hell

The ringing became more distinct: - it continued and
became more distinct: I talked more freely to get rid of
the feeling: but it continued and gained definiteness –
until, at length, I found the noise was not within my
ears.

No doubt I now grew very pale; but I talked more
fluently, and with a heightened voice. Yet the sound
increased - and what could I do? It was a low, dull quick
sound - much such a sound as a watch makes when
enveloped in cotton. I gasped for breath - and yet the
officers heard it not. I talked more quickly -more
vehemently; but the noise steadily increased. I arose and
argued about trifles, in a high key and with violent
gesticulations; but the noise steadily increased. Why
would they not be gone? I paced the floor to and fro
with heavy strides, as if excited to fury by the
observations of the men - but the noise steadily
increased. Oh God! what could I do? I foamed - I
raved - I swore! I swung the chair upon which I had been
sitting, and grated it upon the boards, but the noise
arose over all, and continually increased. It grew louder -
louder – louder! And still the men chatted pleasantly,
and smiled. Was it possible they heard not?

Chapter Four – I heard many things in hell

Almighty God! - no, no! They heard! - they suspected! - they knew! - they were making a mockery of my horror! - this I thought and this I think. But anything was better than this agony! Anything was more tolerable than this derision! I could bear those hypocritical smiles no longer! I felt that I must scream or die? and now —again! - hark! Louder! Louder! Louder! Louder!

"Villains!" I shrieked, "dissemble no more! I admit the deed! - tear up the planks! here, here! it is the beating of his hideous heart!"

"From Space man comes to this foul Planet Earth, to play his part, to enact his scene, - and add his bones to the dust of yore."

Alone

From childhood's hour I have not been
As others were - I have not seen
As others saw - I could not bring
My passions from a common spring
From the same source I have not taken
My sorrow! I could not awaken
My heart to joy at the same tone;
And all I lov'd, I lov'd alone.
Then, - in my childhood - in the dawn
Of a most stormy life - was drawn
From ev'ry depth of good and ill
The mystery which binds me still;
From the torrent, or the fountain,
From the red cliff of the mountain,
From the sun that round me roll'd
In its autumn tint of gold -
From the lightning in the sky
As it pass'd me flying by-
From the thunder and the storm,
And the cloud that took the form
(When the rest of Heaven was blue)
Of a demon in my view.

Chapter Four – I heard many things in hell

Poe - was destined to write tales `with a demon in his view´ and what a pity, they could not earn him a good living. To start with Poe had to supply a Poem and a Tale for each newspaper that he worked for. This meant that he had to churn them out pretty regularly. His articles and reviews were also used to fill up the newspapers that he worked for, - which were more like magazines. So, today, when people read a selection of the tales, they believe that he wrote them for a collection, but, no - oh no´ Poe wrote his tales to `earn a living´ and the poems were also mere means of acquiring food for his `family´. The Tell-Tale Heart, is the best example of Poe's constructed tales, there are others, but this tale has beginning, middle and end and leant itself to the adaptation of Play and Film, - which would have been approved of, I feel sure, by the Master himself.

Chapter Five — 'If you seek for Eldorado'

"As you see, I am not dead, my books are still being read, and it seems that a Premature Burial of my own self was the reason why I never attained greatness or solvency. Such was the nature of my degradation that I died, drunk, delirious and poverty-stricken. I was found lying in the street, in a very bad way. I still don't know what happened to this dying day. You see, Death and I had been playing a game for a whole year; and despite my cheating methods, using laudanum, a poison of my day, neither of us succeeded, and the game ended in a draw. Death, reluctantly, took me into her bosom. On October 7th. 1849, I died.

Died, in the flesh, but, never in the Spirit, I am still a wandering Spirit amongst you all. My Spirit lives on within your being: I am alive, in each and every one of you, in some way. You see, my mind, reached beyond the barriers of Space, and delved into the natural, super-natural of the soul and the mind. The physical being, lost in the physical world, the mind, became loose, and wandered through time and space like a lonely, lost, wandering soul, eternally; never to reach its goal."

Poe's Obituary

Edgar Allan Poe is dead. He died in Baltimore the day before yesterday. This announcement will startle many, but few will be grieved by it. The Poet was well-known personally or by reputation in all of America; he had readers in England and in several of the States of Continental Europe, but he had no friends..........

.........................by Rufus Wilmot Griswold.

The Pit and the Pendulum

. . . . . . .I was sick, sick unto death with that long agony;
and when they at length unbound me, and I was
permitted to sit, I felt that my senses were leaving me.
The sentence - the dread sentence of death - was the
last of distinct accentuation which reached my ears.
After that the sound of the inquisitorial voices seemed
merged in one dreamy indeterminate hum. It conveyed
to my soul the idea of revolution - perhaps with its
association in fancy to the burr of a mill-wheel. This only
for a brief period, for presently I heard no more. Yet,
for a while, I saw - but with how terrible an
exaggeration! I saw the lips of the black-robed judges.
They appeared to me white - whiter than the sheet upon
which I trace these words - and thin even to
grotesqueness; thin with the intensity of their expression
of firmness of immovable resolution - of stern contempt
of human torture. I saw that the decrees of what to me
was fate were still issuing from those lips. I saw them
writhe with a deadly locution. I saw them fashion the
syllables of my name, and I shuddered because no sound
succeeded.

I saw, too, for a few moments of delirious horror, the soft and nearly imperceptible waving of the sable draperies which enwrapped the walls of the apartment. And then my vision fell upon the seven tall candles on the table. At first, they wore the aspect of charity, and seemed white slender angels who would save me; but then, all at once, there came a most deadly nausea over my spirit and I felt every fibre in my frame thrill as if I had touched the wire of a galvanic battery, while the angel forms became meaningless spectres with heads of flame, and I saw that from them there would be no help.

And then there stole into my fancy like a rich musical note, the thought of what sweet rest there must be in the grave. The thought came gently and stealthily and it seemed long before it attained full appreciation; but just as my spirit came at length properly to feel and entertain it, the figures of the judges vanished, as if magically, from before me; the tall candles sank into nothingness; their flames went out utterly; the blackness of darkness supervened; all sensations appeared swallowed up in a mad rushing descent as of the soul into Hades. Then, silence and stillness, and night were the Universe.

Chapter Five – 'If you seek for Eldorado'

For some minutes after this fancy possessed me, I remained without motion. And why? I could not summon courage to move. I dared not make the effort that was to satisfy me of my fate - and yet there was something at my heart which whispered me it was sure. Despair - such as no other species of wretchedness ever calls into being - despair alone urged me, after long irresolution, to uplift the heavy lids of my eyes. I uplifted them. It was dark - all dark. I knew that the fit was over. I knew that the crisis of my disorder was long passed. I knew that I had fully recovered the use of my visual faculties - and yet it was dark - all dark - the intense and utter raylessness of the Night that endureth for evermore.

I endeavoured to shriek; and my lips and my parched tongue moved convulsively together in the attempt but no voice issued from the cavernous lungs, which, oppressed as if by the weight of some incumbent mountain, gasped and palpitated, with the heart, at every elaborate and struggling inspiration.

The movement of the jaws, in this effort to cry aloud, showed me that they were bound up, as is usual with the dead. I felt, too, that I lay upon some hard substance; and by something similar my sides were also closely compressed. So far, I had not ventured to stir any of my limbs - but now I violently threw up my arms, which had been lying at length, with the wrists crossed. They struck a solid wooden substance, which extended above my person at an elevation of not more than six inches from my face. I could no longer doubt that I reposed within a coffin. And now, as if by the rush of an ocean my shuddering spirit is overwhelmed by the one grim danger, by the one spectral and ever-prevalent idea - that I have been buried alive!

The Colloquy of Monos and Una

Prematurely induced by intemperance of knowledge, the old age of the world drew on. This the mass of mankind saw not, or, living lustily although unhappily, affected not to see. But, for myself, the Earth's records had taught me to look for the widest ruin as the price of highest civilisation. I had imbibed a prescience of our Fate from comparison of China the simple and enduring, with Assyria the architect, with Egypt the astrologer, with Nubia, more crafty than either, the turbulent mother of all Arts. In the history of these regions I met with a ray for the future. The individual artificialties of the three latter were local diseases of the Earth, and in their individual overthrows we had seen local remedies applied; but for the infected world at large I could anticipate no regeneration save in death. That man, as a race, should not become extinct, I saw that he must be 'Born Again.'

"My Mother and Father were Leading Actor and Actress in Boston, Massachusetts. I was born on January 19th. 1809.

Chapter Five – 'If you seek for Eldorado'

My name was derived from Shakespeare, as my Father was playing Edmund the Bastard son of Gloucester in 'King Lear'; I, being legitimate was named after the other son, Edgar; 'Poor Tom.'

Mother played Cordelia, and I appeared on stage for several weeks, but was never seen as I was still in my Mother's womb.

Father had taken to drink, it was his undoing, one night he did not appear at all; he was undone. History has no further record of him, but the sins of the father were visited on the son.

Mother moved to New York, taking smaller parts, then, to Richmond, Charleston and Norfolk, finally illness overtook her on Dec. 8th 1811, she died.

So, I was adopted by a Mr. Allan, when I was three. My foster parents were not show-business people, they ran a general store under the cognomen of Ellis and Allan. Their business was a success and it lead to my beginning a costly education.

Chapter Five – 'If you seek for Eldorado'

Despite Mr. Allan's materialistic pursuits, he frequently quoted 'The Bard', and had a store of tales from his own native Scotland. He had been born in Ayr, home of Robert Burns, the Poet.

The war with Great Britain waged until 1815, but as soon as the treaty was signed, Ellis and Allan opened a branch in England. I had attained the age of six!

We took the boat to Liverpool, and although Mother was very sea-sick, Father and I 'spliced the main brace and walked the planks' with the ease of two ancient mariners. We stayed a week in Liverpool, then, on to Scotland and my Father's old haunts. His Scots accent becoming very noticeable when he quoted 'Rabbie Burns' 'Tam O' Shanter', to me.

We travelled around visiting many glorious towns Glasgow, Edinburgh, Newcastle, Sheffield, and finally London. We dwelt at 47, Southampton Row, Russell Square, in the Parish of Bloomsbury.

My father employed a clerk, George Dubourg, who had two sisters that ran a school in Sloane Street, Chelsea. When he heard that his new employer had a seven-year-old son, seeking a school, he deemed that I should be sent to Chelsea.

My step-mother lost her strength in the gloom and fog of London. So, father took her to Cheltenham in Gloucestershire, where she wished to remain.

Now, Father had his hands full, with me at school and Mother in the country. However, he insisted on my going to a more advanced school, as I had done so well at the Dubourgs. (See a reference in "Murders in the Rue Morgue")

William Wilson

My earliest recollections of a school life are connected with a large, rambling, Elizabethan House, in a misty looking village of England, where were a vast number of gigantic and gnarled trees, and where all the houses were excessively ancient.

Chapter Five – 'If you seek for Eldorado'

In truth, it was a dreamlike and spirit-soothing place, that venerable old town, - Stoke Newington.

(Here is Poe's most vivid memory of his youth) The house, I have said, was old and irregular. The grounds were extensive, and a high and solid brick wall topped with a bed of mortar and broken glass, encompassed the whole. This prison-like rampart formed the limit of our domain; beyond it we saw but thrice a week, once every Saturday afternoon, when, attended by two ushers, we were permitted to take brief walks in a body through some of the neighbouring fields, and twice during Sunday when we paraded in the same formal manner to the morning and evening service in the one church of the village.

Of this church the Principal of our school was Pastor. The Reverend Dr. John Bransby M.A. (This was a custom of the time, whereby the principal schoolmaster was the local Pastor, also, - which gave him a six-day week, with only Saturday off.)

Chapter Five – 'If you seek for Eldorado'

With how deep a spirit of wonder and perplexity was I wont to regard him from our remote pew in the gallery, as with step solemn and slow, he ascended the pulpit!

This reverend man, with countenance so demurely benign, with robes so glossy and so clerically flowing, with wig so minutely powdered, so rigid and vast, could this be he who, of late, with sour visage, and in snuffy habiliments, administered, ferule in hand, the Draconian Laws of the Academy? Oh, gigantic paradox too utterly monstrous for solution!

"The boys seemed to dislike me, they mimicked my accent, and once, while playing football a boy trod on my hand, the surgeon's bill came to thirteen shillings.

Latin and French were among my best subjects, and I was well ahead in History and Literature; the Headmaster, however, did not like the constant stream of pocket-money from my Foster-Father.

Business was poor, and Father was down to his last hundred pounds, when I brought home a school-bill of seventy pounds. He decided to return to Richmond.

While the London mobs were unhitching the horses of Queen Carolina's coach, and pulling it themselves, and George IVth was accusing her of high treason; Mother, Father and I, scuttled through the crowds to catch the coach to Liverpool.

The business was saved, as the Tariff Bill did not go through. So, - we set off from Liverpool, on June 14th. 1820. Father with hopeful spirits, Mother, - still her sea-sickly self; then, myself, returning to the country where I was to be known as the writer, *Edgar Allan Poe*.

Eldorado

Gaily bedight,
A gallant knight,
In sunshine and in shadow,
Had journeyed long,
Singing a song,
In search of Eldorado.

But he grew old -
This knight so bold -
And o'er his heart a shadow
Fell as he found
No spot of ground
That looked like Eldorado
And as his strength
Failed him at length
He met a pilgrim shadow -

"Shadow," said he,
"Where can it be -
This land of Eldorado?"
"Over the mountains
Of the moon,

Chapter Five – 'If you seek for Eldorado'

Down the Valley of the Shadow,
Ride, boldly ride,"
The Shade replied: -
"If you seek for Eldorado."

"Over a month at sea, before we returned to the
squalor of New York. We returned to live at Mr.
Ellis's house in Richmond, Virginia.

At school, I was a leader in all subjects, even at bare-
fist fighting. My first attempts at writing came at
thirteen years, as I was an avid reader. Joseph
Clarke, my Schoolmaster discovered an Anthology of
my poetry, while marking my arithmetic. I won first prize
for elocution, and all admired my six-mile swim from
Ludlam's Wharf to Warwick, on the James' River.
1822, Edgar Allan Poe, 13!

The Haunted Palace

In the greenest of our valleys
By good angels tenanted,
Once a fair and stately palace -
Radiant palace - reared its head.
In the monarch thought's dominion -
It stood there!
Never seraph spread a pinion
Over fabric half so fair!

Banners yellow, glorious, golden,
On its roof did float and flow,
(This - all this - was in the olden
Time long ago;)
And every gentle air that dallied,
In that sweet day,
Along the ramparts plumed and pallid,
A winged odour went away.

Wanderers in that happy valley,
Through two luminous windows, saw
Spirits moving musically,
To a lute's well-tuned law,
Round about a throne, where, sitting
(Porphyrogene!)
In state his glory well befitting
The ruler of the realm was seen.

But evil things, in robes of sorrow,
Assailed the monarch's high estate.
(Ah, let us mourn! - for never morrow
Shall dawn upon him desolate!)
And round about his home the glory
That blushed and bloomed
Is but a dim-remembered story
Of the old time entombed.

The Poem is full of optimism at the beginning, but, it
turns to pessimism towards the end. Poe can see his life
as it is going to be. His University days start off well, -
but peter out when John Allan does not help, - the
same at West Point, and when Poe asks for Allan's
help when he is desperately trying to earn from his

Chapter Six – "In Heaven a Spirit doth dwell..."

writings, again, he has to go elsewhere, - then, Poe is in a desperate stage when his Step-Father expires.

"The University and my studies cost many dollars which John Allan refused to pay. Then, I damned myself in a letter to a debtor, by saying that my Foster-Father was seldom sober.... The rift caused was never again breached.

My poverty-stricken weeks in Boston found me selling my only volume of poetry. A few copies were sold, but my name was in print.

Edgar A. Perry was the pseudonym I used to enlist in the Army, stating my age as 22, though, only 18 years had besieged my brow. The siege of my senses was about to begin....

Dream Within a Dream

Take this kiss upon the brow!
And, in parting from you now,
Thus much let me avow -
You are not wrong, who deem
That my days have been a dream!
Yet if hope has flown away
In a night, or in a day,
In a vision, or in none,
Is it therefore the less gone?
All that we see or seem
Is but a dream within a dream.

I stand amid the roar
Of a surf-tormented shore,
And I hold within my hand
Grains of the golden sand -
How few! yet how they creep
Through my fingers to the deep,
While I weep - while I weep!
O God! Can I not grasp
Them with a tighter clasp?
O God! Can I not save

One from the pitiless wave?
Is all that we see or seem
But a dream within a dream?

Dreamland

By a route obscure and lonely,
Haunted by ill-angels only,
Where an Eidolon, named NIGHT,
On a black throne reigns upright,
I have reached these lands but newly
From an ultimate dim Thule -
From a wild weird clime that lieth, sublime,
Out of space -out of TIME.

Poe goes into his Dreamland, and all that he sees is
'A Dream within a Dream.' However, he knows that
his writing is everything, - and, at first, it is the
Poetry, that must come first in spite of everything!

"May, 1829, Baltimore; I see the remains of my family,
a paralytic Grandmother, her daughter Maria
Clemm, widowed with two children, Virginia and
Henry.

Chapter Six – "In Heaven a Spirit doth dwell..."

Henry Poe had used my poems and his own initials, and written on my love for Sarah Elmira Royster.

All avenues were tried for publication of my poems, and Mr. Allan forwarded money, intended for my entry into West Point Military Academy.

I lived economically, and walked fruitlessly to Washington, only to return, because of a lack of finance, and my non-acceptance to West Point.

December, 1829, my first volume of Poetry was published, the reviews were lukewarm, but I was showing my genius in Tamerlane and Al Aaraaf. Mr. Allan invited me over to Richmond, where I was immediately re-clothed, re-housed and re-hosed.

The money was found for West Point, and I left my Virginia home for the last time.

At West Point, I was the eldest, and felt an odd man out with all the youngsters; and I could not stand the drilling.

Chapter Six – "In Heaven a Spirit doth dwell..."

Our rules were rigid, no tobacco, alcohol, or card playing, - even games, plays, and novels were taboo. My education prompted me to walk through Maths and French, but, the money began to run out.

Mr. Allan would not help, and my court martial for certain offences was due. I was turned out of West Point, penniless, with a cold, and an infected ear.

My one belief was predominant. Poetry is the art, my art, God's art. Poetry is for pleasure, poetry is a pleasurable idea put to music. Science, I do not believe in thee. My law, is the law of nature, my code is my work, my prodigious effort, and my ethics are within my art."

Israfel

In Heaven a spirit doth dwell
"Whose heart-strings are a lute."
None sing so wildly well
As the angel Israfel,
And the giddy stars, (so legends tell),
Ceasing their hymns, attend the spell
Of his voice, all mute.

And they say (the starry choir
And the other listening things)
That Israfeli's fire
Is owing to that lyre
By which he sits and sings -
The trembling living wire
Of those unusual strings.

If I could dwell
Where Israfel
Hath dwelt, and he where I
He might not sing so wildly well
A mortal melody
While a bolder note than this might swell
From my lyre within the sky.

Chapter Six – "In Heaven a Spirit doth dwell..."

"The new edition of poems received favourable criticism from the same critics who rejected me, before.

One hundred dollars prize money for the best short story was announced in the Saturday Courier in Baltimore.

At this point in my life, old debtors returned. John Allan was re-marrying Louisa Gabriella Patterson. I was threatened with the possibility of imprisonment, and wrote to my Foster-Father using dignity and humility. After I had spent a miserable Christmas, help arrived early in the New Year. My stories did not win the competition, but were published during that year. This, saved me from the debtors' prison.

I dedicated myself to the pen in hand writer and bachelor of romantic pursuits. Railroads were being built, time was moving forward.

John Allan was ailing, and no more subsistence was forthcoming. My position had reached another desperate stage, when he died, in 1834, leaving me nothing in his Will."

"The Spring however, was the beginning of the change, when another competition was announced.

I should have won all three prizes, but the Editor of 'The Visitor' writing under an assumed name, won the Poetry prize. My Poem, 'The Coliseum' was published later, and the story that gained me my first 100 dollars prize was M.S. Found in a Bottle:"

Of my country and of my family I have little to say. Ill usage and length of years have driven me from one, and estranged me from the other. Hereditary wealth afforded me an education of no common order, and a contemplative turn of mind enabled me to methodise the stories which early study diligently garnered up. Beyond, all things, the works of the German moralists gave me great delight; not from my ill-advised admiration for their eloquent madness, but from the ease with which my habits of rigid thoughts enabled me to detect their falsities. I have often been reproached for the aridity of my genius; a deficiency of imagination has been deputed to me as a crime; and the Pyrrhonism of my opinions has at all times rendered me notorious. Indeed a strong relish for the physical philosophy has, I fear, tinctured

my mind with a very common error of this age - I mean
the habit of referring occurrences, even the least
susceptible of such reference, to the principles of science.
Upon the whole, no person could be less liable than
myself to be led away from the severe precincts of the
truth by the ignes fatui of superstition. I have thought
to premise thus much, lest the incredible tale I have to
tell should be considered rather the ravings of a crude
imagination, than the positive experience of a mind to
which the reveries of fancy have been a dead letter and
a nullity.

"In many productions, terror has been the thesis, I
maintain that terror is not of <u>Germany</u> but, of the
soul.

The horror that went into my stories was the horror
that I felt at the time. In Berenice, I refer to my
cousin, Virginia, likewise in Eleonora, and despite my
incessant love for cats, this feline creature was the
subject of one of my most horrific tales.....

....THE BLACK CAT"

From my infancy I was noted for the docility and humanity of my disposition. My tenderness of heart was even so conspicuous as to make me the jest of my companions. I was especially fond of animals, and was indulged by my parents with a great variety of pets. With these I spent most of my time, and never was so happy as when feeding and caressing them. This peculiarity of character grew with my growth, and, in my manhood I derived from it one of my principle sources of pleasure. To those who have cherished an affection for a faithful and sagacious dog, I need hardly be at the trouble of explaining the nature of the intensity of the gratification thus derivable. There is something in the unselfish and self-sacrificing love of a brute, which goes directly to the heart of him who has had frequent occasion to test the paltry friendship and gossamer fidelity of mere Man.

One night, returning home much intoxicated, from one of my haunts about town, I fancied that the cat avoided my presence. I seized him; when, in his fright at my violence, he inflicted a slight wound upon my hand with his teeth. The fury of a demon instantly possessed me. I knew myself no longer. My original soul seemed, at once, to take its flight from my body; and a more than fiendish malevolence, gin-nurtured, thrilled every fibre of my frame.

I took from my waistcoat-pocket a pen-knife, opened it, grasped the poor beast by the throat, and deliberately cut one of its eyes from the socket I blush, I burn, I shudder, while I pen the damnable atrocity.

When reason returned with the morning - when I had slept off the fumes of the night's debauch - I experienced a sentiment half of horror, half of remorse, for the crime of which I had been guilty; but it was, at best, a feeble and equivocal feeling, and the soul remained untouched. I again plunged into excess, and soon drowned in wine all memory of the dead. In the meantime the cat slowly recovered. The socket of the lost eye presented, it is true, a frightful appearance, but he no longer appeared to suffer any pain. He went about the house as usual, but, as might be expected, fled in extreme terror, at my approach. I had so much of my old heart left, as to be at first grieved by this evident dislike on the part of a creature which had once so loved me. But this feeling soon gave place to irritation. And then came, as if to my final and irrevocable overthrow, the spirit of Perverseness. Of this spirit philosophy takes no account. Yet I am not more sure that my soul lives, than I am that perverseness is one of the primitive impulses of the human heart - one of the indivisible primary faculties or sentiments, which give direction to the character of man. Who has not, a hundred times, found himself committing a vile or silly action, for no other reason than because he knows he should not? Have we not a perpetual inclination, in the teeth of our best judgment to violate that which is law, merely because we understand it to be such? This spirit of perverseness, I say, came to my final overthrow. It was this unfathomable longing for the soul to vex itself - to offer violence to its own nature - to do wrong for the wrong's sake only, - that urged me to continue and finally to consummate the injury I had inflicted upon the unoffending brute.

One morning, in cool blood, I slipped a noose about its neck and hung it to the limb of a tree -hung it with the tears streaming from my eyes, and with the bitterest remorse at my heart - hung it because I knew that it had loved me, and because I felt it had given me no reason of offence; - hung it because I knew that in so doing I was committing a sin - a deadly sin that would so jeopardise my immortal soul as to place it - if such a thing were possible - even beyond the reach of the infinite mercy of the most Merciful and Terrible God.

"The change was coming; but no material gain. It took all my tales to the Folio Club, to raise 15 dollars, so we could enjoy a merry Christmas in 1834. The Southern Literary Messenger printed Hans Phfaal, Berenice and Lionizing, but my unkempt appearance failed me for a teaching job. Once again, an imploring letter, - this time to John Kennedy, publisher. I was invited to his house, fed, clothed and given a horse, - I could have eaten one! He urged me to write whatever would make money, and POLITIAN was therefore shelved."

'Politian' was a Roman Drama that Poe was writing (of all things) at that time. So, it became clear to the young writer that he would have to produce a lot of material to survive, as a writer. He had already realised his ambitions, but the Poetry would not earn him any kind of living on his own.

He realised very early on that he would have to write many tales, just to keep 'the pot boiling'. Even as early as this; Poe knew his destiny, - he recognised his own genius, but tried to deny it. He did in no way relish the physical side of life, in - M.S. this is a mere contradiction. Poe already realised that his future lay in his works, and that he would use it, to express his Life. In 'The Black Cat' Poe again expresses his own nature, and his actual kindness towards cats, rather than what actually happens in the story. Here, in the story, he describes the eccentricities of a drunken man, who did he learn this from: his Foster-Father? He was only three when he lost his real 'drunken' Father. But, what Poe was doing was predicting his own future.

Poe's obsession with death and most of all the death of a beautiful woman, inspired poems and tales that gave Poe one of his most fascinating and compelling traits, - thoughts of necrophilia were there.. .but all...all in the spiritual...sense, for Poe;... for nowhere in Poe's entire works could I find anything salacious!!

Usher - Ligeia, Morella, Eleonora, Berenice and Annabel Lee seem to have been influenced by Virginia, with somewhere in the back of his mind, his gin-drinking Mother coughing blood from her own TB, as well as Virginia and her burst blood vessel.

Poe makes all his heroines beautiful, and Hammer Horror also complemented this in the Dracula films, which followed Corman's introduction of Poe to the Silver Screen. Again, - Poe's influence.

If Poe had been alive today, he would be turning out scripts for TV and Films, I feel sure. However, the editor of the Southern Literary Messenger, did not find his true calling until he owned fifty percent of the Broadway Journal, but this was towards the end of his life. He kept the Journal going almost single-handedly,

Chapter Eight – 'The Passions should be held in reverence'

- but he gained both friends and foes, during 1846, only three years before his death, he was at his most productive.

"Here was my true calling, the man of letters, words, books, and love for life. People were pleased with my manner and my bearing was one of high class."

"A quiet, patient, industrious and most gentlemanly person, commanding the utmost respect and good feeling by his unvarying deportment and ability, his humility and perseverance earned him friendship and admiration, but not love ...."

"Events prevented me from following my true passion. Poetry had been my passion from an early age, and the passions should be held in reverence, they must not, they cannot at will be excited, with an eye to the paltry compensations, or the more paltry commendations of mankind."

The Poetic Principle

The Poetic Sentiment, of course, may develop itself in various modes, in Painting, in Sculpture, in Architecture, in the Dance, Very Especially in Music and very peculiarly, and with a wide field, in the composition of the Landscape Garden. Our present theme, however, has regard only to its manifestation in words. And here let me speak briefly on the topic of rhythm. Contenting myself with the certainty that Music, in its various modes of metre, rhythm, and rhyme, is of so vast a moment in Poetry as never to be wisely rejected - is so vitally important an adjunct, that he is simply silly who declines its assistance, I will not now pause to maintain its absolute essentiality. It is in Music, perhaps, that the soul most nearly attains the great end for which, when inspired by the Poetic Sentiment, it struggles -the creation of supernal beauty. It maybe, indeed, that here this sublime end is, now and then, attained in fact. We are often made to feel, with a shivering delight, that from an earthly harp are stricken notes which cannot have been unfamiliar to the angels. And thus there can be little doubt that in the union of Poetry with Music in its popular sense, we shall find the widest field for the Poetic development. The old Bards and Minnesingers had advantages which we do not possess - and Thomas Moore, singing his own songs, was, in the most legitimate manner, perfecting them as poems.

To recapitulate, then: - I would define, in brief, the poetry of words as The Rhythmical Creation of Beauty. Its sole arbiter is Taste. With the Intellect or with the Conscience, it has only collateral relations. Unless incidentally, it has no concern whatever either with Duty or with Truth.

And in regard to Truth, - if, to be sure, through the attainment of a truth, we are led to perceive a harmony where none was apparent before, we experience, at once, the true poetical effect -but this effect is referable to the harmony alone, and not in the least degree to the truth which merely served to render the harmony manifest.

We shall reach, however, more immediately a distinct conception of what the true Poetry is, by mere reference to a few of the simple elements which induce in the poet himself the true poetical effect. He recognises the ambrosia which nourishes his soul, in the bright orbs that shine in Heaven - in the volutes of the flower - in the clustering of low shrubberies - in the waving of the grain-fields - in the slanting of tall, Eastern trees - in the blue distance of mountains - in the grouping of clouds - in the twinkling of half-hidden brooks - in the gleaming of silver rivers - in the repose of sequestered lakes - in the star-mirroring depths of lonely wells. He perceives it in the songs of birds - in the harp of Aeolus - in the sighing of the night-wind - in the repining voice of the forest - in the surf that complains to the shore - in the fresh breath of the woods - in the scent of the violet - in the voluptuous perfume of the hyacinth - in the suggestive odour that comes to him, at eventide, from far-distant, undiscovered islands, over dim oceans, illimitable and unexplored. He owns it in all noble thoughts - in all unworldly motives - in all holy impulses - in all chivalrous, generous, and self-sacrificing deeds.

He feels it in the beauty of woman - in the grace of her step - in the lustre of her eye - in the melody of her voice - in her soft laughter - in her sigh - in the harmony of the rustling of her robes. He deeply feels it in her winning

Chapter Eight – 'The Passions should be held in reverence'

endearments - in her burning enthusiasms - in her gentle
charities - in her meek and devotional endurances but
above all - ah, far above all - he kneels to it - he worships
it in the faith, in the purity, in the strength, in the
altogether divine majesty - of her love.

What writer would explain <u>How</u> he creates poetry with
such style, Poe relates the influences that affect the
Poet, himself. No other Poet has gone into his art so
deeply. Power to his elbow; Poe was not afraid of
Truth, but he knew the other people would put a veil
over it. Hence, he himself, lived in his own world and the
every day life, - to Poe, it was 'the hideous dropping
off, of the veil.'

The General Proposition is this: Because nothing <u>was</u>, therefore all things <u>are</u>.

1. An inspection of the Universality of Gravitation i.e. of the fact that each particle tends, not to any one common point, but, to every other particle suggests <u>perfect totality</u> or <u>absolute unity</u> as the source of the phenomenon.

2. Gravity is but the mode in which is manifested the tendency of all things to return to the original unity - is but the reaction of the first <u>Divine Act</u>.

3. The Law regulating the return i.e. The Law of Gravitation is but a necessary result of the necessary and sole possible mode of equable irradiation of matter through space.

4. The Universe of Stars (contradistinguished from the Universe of Space) is limited.

5. Mind is cognizant of Matter, only through its two properties, <u>attraction</u> and <u>repulsion</u>: therefore Matter is only <u>attraction</u> and <u>repulsion</u> a finally consolidated globe of globes, being but one particle, would be without <u>attraction</u> i.e. gravitation: the existence of such a globe presupposed the expulsion of the separate ether which we know to exist between the particles as at present diffused, thus the final globe would be matter without attraction and repulsion: but these are matter: then the final globe would be matter without matter, i.e. no matter at all, it must disappear. This <u>Unity</u> is nothingness.

6. Matter springing from Unity sprang from Nothingness i.e. was created.

7. All will return to Nothingness, in returning to Unity.... What I have propounded will (in good time) revolutionize the World of Physical and Metaphysical Science. I say this calmly <u>but I say it</u>.

Chapter Nine — The 'Eureka' Episode

Poe wrote Eureka towards the end of his life, and although he believed it to be his finest work; having finished it, - all he wanted to do was die. However, there were still possibilities with The Stylus; and Griswold was to gather up his entire works, surely this would bring him the fame he so desperately alluded to. He was known for his Tales of Mystery and Imagination, his Tales of Terror; his Poem The Raven came late in his career, and he devoted his energies to the Broadway Journal. A letter came offering him the chance of his own magazine, - the money did not arrive, but a meeting was for mid-October; he died on October 7th. Poe left a forward with Eureka, stating that he would like it to be accepted as a poem.

To the few who love me and whom I love - to those who feel rather than to those who think - to the dreamers and those who put faith in dreams as in the only realities - I offer this Book of Truths, not in its character of Truth-Teller, but for the beauty that abounds in its truth - constituting it true. To these I present the composition as an Art-Product alone, - let us say as a Romance, or, if I be not urging too, lofty a claim, as a Poem.

Chapter Nine – The 'Eureka' Episode

What I here propound is true: therefore it cannot die: or if by any means it be now trodden down so that it dies, it will rise again to the Life Everlasting.

Nevertheless, it is as a poem only that I wish this work to be judged after I am dead.

There was an epoch in the night of time, when a still-existent Being existed - one of an absolutely infinite number of similar Beings that people the absolutely infinite domains of the absolutely infinite space. It was not and is not in the power of this Being - any more than it is in your own - to extend by actual increase, the joy of his Existence; - but.... this Divine Being...passes his eternity in perpetual variation of Concentrated Self and almost Infinite Self-Diffusion. What you call The Universe is but his present expansive existence.... All these creatures (in the Universe) – all - those which you term animate, as well to whom you deny life for no better reason than you do not behold it in operation - all these creatures have, in a greater or less degree, a capacity for pleasure and for pain: - but the general sum of their sensations is precisely that amount of Happiness which appertains by right to the Divine Being when concentrated within Himself. These creatures are all, too, more or less conscious Intelligences; conscious, first, of a proper identity; conscious…by faint indeterminate glimpses of an identity with the Divine Being of whom we speak - of an identity with God. Of the two classes of consciousness fancy that the former will grow weaker, and the latter stronger, during the long succession of ages which must elapse before these myriads of intelligences become blended into One. Think…that Man, for example, ceasing imperceptibly to feel himself Man, will at length attain that awfully triumphant epoch when he shall recognise his existence with that of Jehovah. In the meantime bear in mind that all is Life - Life - Life within Life - the less within the greater, and all within the spirit Divine.

….We walk about, amid the destinies of our world-existence, encompassed by dim but ever present memories of a Destiny more vast - very distant in the bygone time, and infinitely awful.

Chapter Nine – The 'Eureka' Episode

We live out a youth peculiarly haunted by such dreams; yet never mistaking them for dreams. As memories we know them…

So long as this youth endures, the feeling that we exist is the most natural of all feelings…

That there was a period at which we did not exist - or that it might so have happened that we never had existed at all - are the considerations, indeed, which during this youth, we find difficulty in understanding. Why we should not exist, is, up to the epoch of our Manhood, of all queries the most unanswerable. Existence - self-existence - existence from all Time and to all eternity - seems, up to the epoch of Manhood, a normal and unquestionable condition - seems, because it is.

The pain of the consideration that we shall lose our individual identity ceases at once when we reflect that our aspirations are merely the absorption by each individual intelligence, of all other intelligences (that is, of the Universe) into its own. That God may be all in all, each must become God.

Chapter Nine – The 'Eureka' Episode

And the will therein lieth, which dieth not. Who knoweth the mysteries of the will, with its vigour? For God is but a great will pervading all things by nature of its intentness. Man doth not yield himself to the angels, or unto death utterly, save only through the weakness of his feeble will.

"June 1839. My intellectual standards were far above the Gentleman's Magazine, run by William E. Burton, - the Actor. Having built up the circulation, I declined after Burton's failure to give me a rise.

I volunteered to campaign for the Whig Party. My Prospectus for the Penn Magazine was complete: this was to be my very own magazine, with World-Wide appeal.

The work, proved too much and the drink to hand consumed; illness struck me down. Penn Magazine postponed until March 1st 1841. By the way, The Whigs won Pennsylvania!"

Literary Life of Thingumbob

How I laboured - how I toiled - how I wrote! Ye Gods, did I not write? I knew not the word 'ease'. By day I adhered to my desk and at night a pale student, I consumed the midnight oil. You should have seen me, you should'. I leaned to the right. I leaned to the left. I sat forward. I sat backward. I sat upon end. I sat tête baisée, bowing my head closer to the alabaster page.

And .... through good report, and through ill report, I wrote. Through sunshine and through moonshine, - I wrote. What I wrote is unnecessary to say. The Style! that was the thing!...

"1841-1842. The very best year, work, work, food, comfort, and no debts. Graham's Magazine and the Saturday Evening Post shared offices and I contributed to both."

Despite Poe resigning from the Gentleman's Magazine; Mr. Burton, it is said, did ask Graham to 'look after' his 'bright young editor' - which Graham (God bless him) did!

The happiest day - the happiest hour
Mine eyes shall see, - have ever seen,
The brightest glance of pride and power
I feel- have been

Chapter Ten — 'rather than the drink to the insanity'

Poe was 33, and there were now to come five years of hopelessness and despair that would scar him inwardly for his last seven years. In a letter to an admirer, he describes about 'The Terrible Evil' - circumstances beyond his control, which forced him to take to the drink for some comfort away from his 'dying' wife.

(To the Admirer) You say, 'Can you hint to me what was the terrible evil which caused the irregularities so profoundly lamented?

(Poe writes in reply)

Yes, I can do more than hint. This 'evil' was the greatest that can befall a man. Six years ago, a wife, whom I loved as no man ever loved before, ruptured a blood vessel in singing. Her life was despaired of. I took leave of her forever, and underwent all the agonies of her death. She recovered partially and I again hoped. At the end of the year, the vessel broke again. I went through precisely the same scene. Again about a year afterward. Then again - again - again, and even once again, at varying intervals. Each time I felt all the agonies of her death - and at each accession of the

Chapter Ten — 'rather than the drink to the insanity'

disorder I loved her more dearly and clung to her life with more desperate pertinacity. But I am constitutionally sensitive - nervous in a very unusual degree. I became insane, with long intervals of horrible sanity. During these fits of absolute unconsciousness, I drank, - God only knows how often or how much. As a matter of course my enemies referred the insanity to the drink rather than the drink to the insanity.

Chapter Eleven – 'the Bird, beat the Bug, all hollow.'

"1843, The Stylus, was the new title for my own magazine. Thomas C. Clarke inserted my biography in the Saturday Museum, to my disapproval.

An attempt at a political career was spent soliciting subscriptions for the Stylus, while on a merry binge with friend 'Rowdy' Dow; - this was not a great success.

The writing took another turn, when 'The Gold Bug' won me a prize of 50 dollars, after I retrieved it from Graham, who had paid his usual fee. It was adapted as a play by Silas S. Steele, and presented at the Walnut Street Theatre on August 8th. 1843.

Potential subscribers and contributors were gathered for 'The Stylus' when I quarreled with Clarke, and all backing was withdrawn. 1844, My Lectures were my latest calling, and lack of opportunity in Philadelphia afforded a return to New York."

The Balloon-Hoax

The last nine hours have been unquestionably the most exciting of my life. I can conceive nothing more sublimating than the strange peril and novelty of an adventure such as this. May God grant that we succeed! I ask not success for mere safety to my insignificant person, but for the sake of human knowledge and - for the vastness of the triumph. And yet the feat is only so evidently feasible that the sole wonder is why men have scrupled to attempt it before. One single gale such as now befriends us - let such a tempest whirl forward a balloon for four or five days (these gales often last longer) and the voyager will be easily borne, in that period, from coast to coast. In view of such a gale the broad Atlantic becomes a mere lake. I am more struck; just now, notwithstanding its agitation, than with any other phenomenon presenting itself.

The waters give up no voice to the heavens. The immense flaming ocean writhes and is tortured uncomplainingly.

Chapter Eleven – 'the Bird, beat the Bug, all hollow.'

The mountainous surges suggest the idea of innumerable dumb gigantic fiends struggling in impotent agony.

In a night such as this to me, a man lives, - lives a whole century of ordinary life - nor would I forego this rapturous delight for that of a whole century of ordinary existence.

"Prepared for my trip to New York was 'The Balloon Hoax' and after a good breakfast at the boarding-house in Greenwich Street, I left with four dollars and fifty cents in my pocket. The story was introduced as Headline News and sold at half-a-dollar, and even a shilling a copy.

I contributed articles and reviews, then in the summer we moved to a Farmhouse, where I spent many days dreaming, rambling, and scribbling. It was here that I carefully and meticulously constructed "The Raven" a resounding success; - the bird beat the bug, all hollow."

Chapter Eleven – 'the Bird, beat the Bug, all hollow.'

The Raven

Once upon a midnight dreary, while I pondered,
    weak and weary,
Over many a quaint and curious volume of forgotten
    lore,
While I nodded, nearly napping, suddenly there came
    a tapping,
As of someone gently rapping, rapping at my chamber
    door.
"'Tis some visitor," I muttered, "tapping at my
    chamber door -
Only this, and nothing more!"
Presently my soul grew stronger; hesitating then no
    longer
"Sir," said I, "or Madam, truly your forgiveness I
    implore;
But the fact is I was napping, and so gently you came
    rapping,
And so faintly you came tapping, tapping at my
    chamber door,
That I scarce was sure I heard you" - here I opened wide
    the door;-
    Darkness there and nothing more.

Chapter Eleven – 'the Bird, beat the Bug, all hollow.'

Back into the chamber turning, all my soul within me
    burning.
Soon again I heard a tapping somewhat louder than
    before.
"Surely," said I, "surely that is something at my
    window-lattice;
Let me see, then, what thereat is, and this mystery
    explore -
Let my heart be still a moment and this mystery
    explore;-
'Tis the wind and nothing more'"

Open here I flung the shutter, when, with many a flirt
    and flutter,
In there stepped a stately raven of the saintly days of
    yore.
Not the least obeisance made he; not an instant stopped
    or stayed he;
But, with mien of Lord or Lady, perched above my
chamber door
Perched upon a bust of Pallas just above my chamber
door
Perched, and sat, and nothing more.

Chapter Eleven – 'the Bird, beat the Bug, all hollow.'

Then this ebony bird beguiling my sad fancy into smiling,
By the grave and stern decorum of the countenance it
        wore,
"Though thy crest be shorn and shaven, thou, I
        said, "art sure no craven."
Ghastly grim and ancient raven wandering from the
    Nightly shore -
Tell me what thy lordly name is on the Night's
        Plutonian shore!"
        Quoth the raven, "Nevermore!"

And the raven, never flitting, still is sitting, still is
        sitting
On the pallid bust of Pallas just above my chamber
        door;
And his eyes have all the seeming of a demon's that
        is dreaming.
And the lamp-light o'er him streaming throws his
        shadow on the floor;
And my soul from out that shadow that lies floating
        on the floor
Shall be lifted - nevermore!

Chapter Eleven – 'the Bird, beat the Bug, all hollow.'

Following up 'The Balloon Hoax,' this was Poe's greatest success, and he conveyed how the poem was constructed in the 'The Philosophy of Composition.' Any student of Poe should obviously, read the whole poem as well as learn about the construction; but our next chapter deals with Poe's true ambition, to run his own magazine, and he almost achieves this with 'The Broadway Journal.'

Chapter Thirteen — 'nipped in the bud'

"'The Raven' gained me a contract with John Bisco, as co-editor with Charles F. Briggs on the Broadway Journal, the nearest thing to having a magazine of my own. 'The Gold Bug', was translated into French, 'Murders in the Rue Morgue', a year later.

My literary disparagement of Longfellow's Works, and his claim of plagiarism against me, blew up into a verbal battle which left a final slur on myself. This did not deter my lectures, nor my contributions to Godey's, Graham's, the American Review and the Journal. (Poe's prolificacy is strongly apparent, during this time.)

Henry C. Watson became my partner when the Bisco and Briggs backing departed, now making my share of the journal fifty percent, - even nearer my dream!

Here was my true calling, the man of letters, words, books and love for life.

Chapter Thirteen — 'nipped in the bud'

However, in 1845, funds were running low, circulation was not high enough to meet rising costs, and early in 1846, I wrote my valedictory to the Journal, bidding farewell, as cordially to friends as to foes.

The War of the Literati was on; New York was the Battlefield, Clarke and Thomas Dunn English led the foray against me. I riposted by writing and criticising with my own ferocity, winning the battle and 225 dollars in costs.

This boost to 1847 was not the beginning of a good year. My own illness was stemming my flow of work, and Virginia was on her last lap of the struggle with life and death. At the end of January, Virginia waned, and finally died."

Annabel Lee

It was many and many a year ago,
In a kingdom by the sea,
That a maiden there lived whom you may know
By the name of Annabel Lee
And this maiden she lived with no other thought
Than to love and be loved by me.

I was a child and she was a child,
In this kingdom by the sea:
But we loved with a love that was more than love
I and my ANNABEL LEE;
With a love that the winged seraphs of heaven
Coveted her and me.

And this was the reason that, long ago,
In this kingdom by the sea,
A wind blew out of a cloud, chilling
My beautiful Annabel Lee;
So that her highborn kinsmen came
And bore her away from me,
To shut her up in a sepulchre
In this kingdom by the sea.

Chapter Thirteen – 'nipped in the bud'

The angels, not half so happy in heaven,
Went envying her and me
Yes! that was the reason (as all men know
In this kingdom by the sea)
That the wind came out of the cloud by night
Chilling and killing my ANNABEL LEE!

But our love it was stronger by far than the love
Of those who were older than we -
Of many far wiser than we -
And neither the angels in heaven above
Nor the demons down under the sea,
Can ever dissever my soul from the soul
Of the beautiful Annabel Lee!

For the moon never beams, without bringing me dreams
Of the beautiful Annabel Lee;
And the stars never rise, but I feel the bright eyes
Of the beautiful Annabel Lee;
And so, all the night-tide, I lie down by the side
Of my darling - my darling, my life and my bride,
In her sepulchre there by the sea,
In her tomb by the sounding sea.

"Deep in Earth my love is lying, and I must weep alone."

Chapter Thirteen — `nipped in the bud`

"Now, I began work on the greatest effort of my life,
Eureka! My debts continued despite my flow of work to
Graham's magazine. 1848, and my comeback was
prevalent, I attempted to resurrect the Stylus, and
from a suggestion created `The Bells', my most
rhythmical poem........."

The Bells

Hear the sledges with the bells,
Silver bells!
What a world of merriment their melody foretells
How they tinkle, tinkle, tinkle
In the icy air of night.
While the stars, that oversprinkle
All the heavens seem to twinkle
With a crystalline delight;
Keeping time, time, time,
In a sort of runic rhyme,
To the tintinabulation that so musically wells
From the bells, bells, bells, bells
Bells, bells bells -
From the jingling and the tinkling of the bells.

Chapter Thirteen — 'nipped in the bud'

"Sarah Helen Whitman, my new love, inspired more poems. I was launched again on my literary career, and women charmed to me, especially widows.

My lecture at Wentworth Hall, on the Poets and Poetry of America was a great success.

Another flame crossed my path, Mrs Nancy Richmond, who became my "Annie."

On a spree, I challenged John M. Daniel to a duel. Later, when sober contributed to his paper, The Examiner.

My affair with Sarah Helen Whitman was fleeting and fatuous, more a flight of fancy, than a lasting root. My love for Mrs Richmond was stronger, but she could not and would not leave her husband and daughter for me..."

Chapter Thirteen — `nipped in the bud`

"On one occasion my love drove me to take laudanum, which did not have the desired effect. Instead of killing me, it made me vomit and I was ill afterwards.

Mrs Whitman was warned against meeting me, but her mother persuaded her to marry me. By now, I had turned my affections towards Annie. I tried the Stylus, yet again, as an alternative to marriage."

Hear the mellow wedding bells,
Golden Bells!
What a world of happiness their harmony foretells.
Through the balmy air of night
How they ring out their delight!
From the molten-golden notes,
And all in tune,
What a liquid ditty floats
To the turtle-dove that listens, while she gloats,
On the moon`

Chapter Thirteen – 'nipped in the bud'

"The marriage was arranged for a Monday and we were to return to Mrs Clemm at Fordham, on the Tuesday. Someone tipped Helen with a note about my 'early morning nips,' and the engagement was 'nipped in the bud'. She broke it off, immediately, and was a constant embarrassment to me, until my death."

Hear the loud alarum bells -
Brazen bells!
What a tale of terror now, their turbulency tells!
In the startled ear of night
How they scream out their affright!
Too much horrified to speak,
They can only shriek, shriek,
Out of tune.

Chapter Fourteen – 'I shall not fail, to meet thee in that hollow vale' or 'But where meantime, was the soul?'

"Away from Providence, and the emotional dizziness of female suitors, I started my final year with a burst of creativity.

Circulating all the newspapers, I made the name of Poe; famous.

Inspiration followed in a late-arriving letter from Edward H. N. Patterson, who wished to publish his own magazine, with myself as editor, - the Stylus, - at last!

The money was not forthcoming and I continued my vain pursuit of Annie. A heat wave struck New York, and illness hit my pen. Eureka completed my only wish was to die, it is pain to live, but bliss to die."

(Letter to Mrs Maria Clemm) July 7th 1849

My dear, dear MOTHER,

I have been so ill - have had the cholera, or spasms quite as bad, and can now hardly hold the pen.

The very instant you get this, come to me. The joy of seeing you will almost compensate for our sorrows. We can but die together. It is no use to reason with me now; I must die. I have no desire to live since I have done "Eureka". I could accomplish nothing more. For your sake it would be sweet to live, but we must die together. You have been all in all to me, darling, ever beloved mother, and dearest, truest friend.

I was never really insane, except on occasions where my heart was touched.

I have been taken to prison once since I came here for getting drunk; but then I was not. It was about Virginia.

"I was now a lonely rat in a city of evil. Men sought my life and pain and doubt rendered my brain barren. Saved, by my friends, Barr and Lippard, who put money in my pocket and sent me to Baltimore; I found torment my only friend in Philadelphia; illness from food-poisoning, and deterioration of health showed me I was taking the final path.

Stay for me there, I shall not fail,
To meet thee in that hollow vale."

The Premature Burial

To be buried alive is, beyond question, the most terrific of extremes which has ever fallen to the lot of mere mortality. That it has frequently, very frequently, so fallen will scarcely be denied by those who think. The boundaries which divide Life and Death are at best shadowy and vague. Who shall say where the one ends and where the other begins? We know that there are diseases in which occur total cessations of all apparent functions of vitality, and yet which these cessations are merely suspensions, properly so called.

Chapter Fourteen – 'I shall not fail, to meet thee in that hollow vale' or 'But where meantime, was the soul?'

They are only temporary pauses in the incomprehensible mechanism. A certain period elapses, and some mysterious principle again sets in motion the magic pinions and the wizard wheels. The silver cord was not for ever loosed, nor the golden bowl irreparably broken. But where, meantime, was the soul?

Fearful indeed the suspicion - but more fearful the doom! It may be asserted, without hesitation, that no event is so terribly well adapted to inspire the supremeness of bodily and of mental distress, as is burial before death.

The unendurable oppression of the lungs - the stifling fumes of the damp earth - the clinging to the death garments - the rigid embrace of the narrow house - the blackness of absolute night - the silence like a sea that overwhelms - the unseen palpable presence of the Conqueror Worm - these things, with the thoughts of the air and grass above, with memory of dear friends who would fly to save us if but informed of our fate, and with consciousness that of this fate, they can never be informed - that our hopeless portion is that of the really

Chapter Fourteen — `I shall not fail, to meet thee in that hollow vale' or `But where meantime, was the soul?'

dead -these considerations, I say, carry into the heart, which still palpitates, a degree of appalling and intolerable horror from which the most daring imagination must recoil. We know of nothing so agonising on Earth - we can dream of nothing half so hideous in the realms of the nethermost Hell.

Poe's description of being `Buried Alive,' gave `birth' to many tales of the `undead'; he, himself was fascinated by the subject, and many authors that came after him, probably best known - Bram Stoker of `Dracula' fame.

Chapter Fourteen – 'I shall not fail, to meet thee in that hollow vale' or 'But where meantime, was the soul?'

However, Poe was on a downward spiral towards his death, and what is more, - Poe knew it; even though everything was coming together for him: -he had lectures to deliver; Rufus W. Griswold was gathering up his entire works for publication; there was still a chance of The Stylus becoming a 3-Dollar, (instead of a 5-Dollar) paper; and above all: ah! far above all; Poe had arranged to marry his former first sweetheart, the widowed Sarah Elmira Shelton: - all was set fair for Poe's 'happy ending' but, no; - he was now on his final descent - into The Maelstrom.

Chapter Fifteen – `A Descent in to the Maelstrom´

As I felt the sickening sweep of the descent, I had instinctively tightened my hold upon the barrel, and closed my eyes. For some seconds I dared not open them - while I expected instant destruction, and wondered that I was not already in my death-struggles with the water. But moment after moment elapsed. I still lived. The sense of falling had ceased; and the motion of the vessel seemed much as it had been before, while in the belt of the foam, with the exception that now she lay more along. I took courage and looked once again upon the scene.

Never shall I forget the sensation of awe, horror, and admiration with which I gazed about me. The boat appeared to be hanging, as if by magic, midway down, upon the interior surface of a funnel vast in circumference, prodigious in depth, and whose perfectly smooth sides might have been mistaken for ebony, but for the bewildering rapidity with which they spun around and for the gleaming and ghastly radiance they shot forth, as the rays of the full moon, from that circular rift amid the clouds which I have already described, streamed in a flood of golden glory along the black walls, and far away down into the inmost recesses of the abyss.

Our first slide into the abyss itself, from the belt of
foam above, had carried us to a great distance down
the slope; but our farther descent was by no means
proportionate. Round and round we swept - not with any
uniform movement - but in dizzying swings and jerks,
that sent us sometimes only a few hundred yards -
sometimes nearly the complete circuit of the whirl. Our
progress downward at each revolution, was slow, but
very perceptible.

It was not a new terror that now affected me, but the
dawn of a more exciting hope. This hope arose partly
from memory and partly from present observation. I no
longer hesitated what to do. I resolved to lash myself
securely to the water cask upon which I now held, to cut
it loose from the counter, and throw myself with it into
the water. I attracted my brother's attention by signs,
pointed to the floating barrels that came near us, and
did everything in my power to make him understand
what I was about to do. I thought at length that he
comprehended my design - but, whether this was the case
or not, he shook his head despairingly, and refused to

move from his station by the ring-bolt. It was impossible to reach him; the emergency admitted of no delay; and so, with a bitter struggle, I resigned him to his fate, fastened myself to the cask by means of the lashings which secured it to the counter, and precipitated myself with it, into the sea, without another moment's hesitation.

It might have been an hour, or thereabout, after my quitting the smack, when, having descended to a vast distance beneath me, it made three or four wild gyrations in rapid succession, and, bearing my brother with it, plunged headlong, at once and forever, into the chaos of foam below. The barrel to which I was attached sunk very little farther than half the distance between the bottom of the gulf and the spot at which, I leaped overboard, before a great change took place in the character of the whirlpool. The slope of the sides of the vast funnel became momently less and less steep. The gyrations of the whirl, grew, gradually, less and less violent. By degrees, the froth and the rainbow disappeared, and the bottom of the gulf seemed slowly to uprise. The sky was clear, the winds had gone down, and the full moon was setting radiantly in the west, when I found myself on the surface of the ocean, in full view of the shores of Lofoden and above the spot where the pool of the Moskoe-strom had been.

A boat picked me up - exhausted from fatigue - and (now that the danger was removed) speechless from the memory of its horror. Those who drew me on board were my old mates and daily companions - but they knew me no more than they would have known a traveller from the spirit-land. My hair, which had been raven black the day before, was as white as you see it now. They say too that the whole expression of my countenance had changed. I told them my story - they did not believe it. I now tell it to you - and I can scarcely expect you to put more faith in it than did the merry fishermen of Lofoden.

Poe survives the whirlpool, and his own description makes us accept that not only was Poe there, - but we were also strapped to the barrel, with him. Poe, also has to survive 'The Fall of the House of Usher' Lady Madeline has come from the grave to collect her brother (for burying her too soon). Once again, Poe escapes but to what!?

The Fall of the House of Usher

'Not hear it? - yes, I hear it, and have heard it. Long
-long - long - many minutes, many hours, many days, have
I heard it - yet dared not - oh pity me, miserable wretch
that I am! - I dared not -I dared not speak! We have
put her living in the tomb! Said I not that my senses
were acute? I now tell you that I heard her first feeble
movements in the hollow coffin. I heard them — many,
many days ago - yet I dared not -I dared not speak'
And now - tonight — Ethelred! ha! ha! - the breaking
of the hermit's door, and the death-cry of the dragon,
and the clangour of the shield! - say, rather, the
rending of her coffin, and the grating of the iron hinges
of her prison, and her struggles within the coppered
archway of the vault! Oh whither shall I fly? Will she
not be here anon? Is she not hurrying to upbraid me for
my haste? Have I not heard her footstep on the stair?

Do I not distinguish that heavy and horrible beating of
her heart? "MADMAN! I TELL YOU
THAT SHE NOW STANDS
WITHOUT THE DOOR!"

Chapter Fifteen – `A Descent in to the Maelstrom´

As if in the superhuman energy of his utterance there had been found the potency of a spell - the huge antique panels to which the speaker pointed, threw slowly back, upon the instant, their ponderous and ebony jaws. It was the work of the rushing gust - but then without those doors DID stand the lofty and enshrouded figure of the Lady Madeline of Usher. There was blood upon her white robes, and the evidence of some bitter struggle upon every portion of her emaciated frame. For a moment she remained trembling and reeling to and fro upon the threshold, then, with a low moaning cry, fell heavily inward upon the person of her brother, and in her violent and now final death-agonies, bore him to the floor a corpse, and a victim to the terrors he had anticipated.

From that chamber, and from that mansion, I fled aghast. The storm was still abroad in all it's wrath as I found myself crossing the old causeway. Suddenly there shot along the path a wild light, and turned to see whence a gleam so unusual could have issued; for the vast house and its shadows were alone behind me. The radiance was that of the full, setting, and blood-red moon which now shone vividly though that once barely-

Chapter Fifteen – 'A Descent in to the Maelstrom'

discernible fissure of which I have before spoken as
extending from the roof of the building, in a zig-zag
direction, to the base. While I gazed, this fissure
rapidly widened - there came a fierce breath of the
whirlwind - the entire orb of the satellite burst at once
upon my sight - my brain reeled as I saw the mighty walls
rushing asunder - there was a tumultuous shouting sound
like the voice of a thousand waters - and the deep and
dank tarn at my feet closed sullenly and silently over the
fragments of the "HOUSE OF USHER".

Chapter Sixteen – 'But there was to be no more dallying with the King of Terrors'

Having survived the descent into the maelstrom, and Lady Madeline's grasping hands, Poe still had to go through the Inquisitorial Proceedings, - who had already pronounced his death! Poe was in his final nightmare dream!! He was in the last few months of his life, it was one nightmare after another, until his final death-struggles in the hospital when he deliriously lived some of his own tales of terror. Until, finally - he died with a last gasp - to God - his maker, whom he did not believe in; and made his final peace.

"It was 1849. There was only a fading chance of the Stylus becoming a 3-dollar instead of a 5-dollar paper, the middle of October was settled for a meeting. I continued with the lectures when health prevailed and turned down invitations, due to my lack of a dress coat.

Richmond was to be my final home, fatally in the State of Virginia. Sarah Elmira Shelton, my first love, returned to be my last love. I hoped for another marriage. Rufus W. Griswold, my old publisher, gathered up my entire works for publication, and I joined the Richmond High Society.

I set out on my final trip to New York, with a premonition that I would never see Elmira again. My final party at Sadlers' restaurant was a gay affair, I left, donned in a palm-leaf hat, and clutching a malacca cane. My movements from then on were oblivious, even to myself. I was taken into hospital on October 3rd, and after many ravings died in a delirium on October 7th."

"No Sir; they who saw me what I was shall never see me as I am."

"I had been found unconscious, in ragged attire, lying in the street, clutching a malacca cane."

The Pit and the Pendulum

So far, I had not opened my eyes. I felt that I lay upon my back, unbound, I reached out my hand, and it fell heavily upon something damp and hard. There I suffered it to remain for many minutes, while I strove to imagine where and what I could be. I longed, yet dared not, to employ my vision.

Chapter Sixteen – 'But there was to be no more dallying with the King of Terrors'

I dreaded the first glance at objects around me. It was not that I feared to look upon things horrible, but that I grew aghast lest there should be nothing to see. At length, with a wild desperation at heart, I quickly unclosed my eyes. My worst thoughts, then, were confirmed. The blackness of eternal night encompassed me. I struggled for breath. The intensity of the darkness seemed to oppress and stifle me. The atmosphere was intolerably close. I still lay quietly, and made effort to exercise my reason. I brought to mind the inquisitorial proceedings, and attempted from that point to deduce my real condition. The sentence had passed; and it appeared to me that a very long interval had since elapsed. Yet not for a moment did I suppose myself actually dead. Such a supposition, notwithstanding what we read in fiction, is altogether inconsistent with real existence: -but where and in what state was I?

My outstretched hands at length encountered some solid obstruction. It was a wall, seemingly of stone masonry - very smooth, slimy, - and cold.

Chapter Sixteen – 'But there was to be no more dallying with the King of Terrors'

I followed it up; stepping with all the careful distrust with which certain antique narratives had inspired me. The ground was moist and slippery. I staggered onward for some time, when I stumbled and fell. My excessive fatigue induced me to remain prostrate; and sleep soon overtook me as I lay.

As I arose from the attempt, the mystery of the alteration in the chamber broke at once upon my understanding. I had observed that, although the outlines of the figures upon the walls were sufficiently distinct, yet the colours seemed blurred and indefinite. These colours had now assumed, and were momentarily assuming, a startling and most intense brilliancy, that gave way to the spectral and fiendish portraitures an aspect that might have thrilled even firmer nerves than my own. Demon eyes, of a wild and ghastly vivacity, glared upon me in a thousand directions, where none had been visible before, and gleamed with a lurid lustre of a fire that I could not force my imagination to regard as unreal.

Chapter Sixteen – 'But there was to be no more dallying with the King of Terrors'

Unreal! Even while I breathed there came to my nostrils the breath of the vapour of heated iron!

A suffocating odour pervaded the prison! A deeper glow settled each moment in the eyes that glared at my agonies! A richer tint of crimson diffused itself over the pictured horrors of blood. I panted, I gasped for breath! There could be no doubt of the design of my tormentors! Oh! most unrelenting! Oh most demoniac of men! I shrank from the glowing metal to the centre of the cell.

The heat rapidly increased, and once again I looked up shuddering as with a fit of the ague. There had been a second change in the cell, and now the change was obviously in the form. As before, it was in vain that I first endeavoured to appreciate or understand what was taking place. But not long was I left in doubt. The inquisitorial vengeance had been hurried by my two-fold escape from the Pit and the Pendulum. But there was to be no more dallying with the King of Terrors.

Chapter Sixteen – 'But there was to be no more dallying with the King of Terrors'

The room had been square, I saw that two of its iron angles were now acute, two consequently obtuse. The fearful difference quickly increased with a low rumbling sound. In an instant the apartment had shifted its form into that of a lozenge. But the alteration stopped not there - I neither hoped nor desired it to stop.

I could have clasped the red walls to my bosom as a garment of eternal peace. "Death" I said, "any death but that of the Pit!" 'Fool', might I not have known that into the pit it was the object of the burning iron to urge me? Could I resist its glow? or even if that, could I withstand its pressure? And now, flatter, and flatter grew the lozenge, with a rapidity that left me no time for contemplation. Its centre and of course its greatest width, came just over the yawning gulf. I shrank back - but the closing walls pressed me resistlessly onward. At length for my seared and writhing body there was no longer an inch of foothold on the firm floor of the prison, I struggled no more, but the agony of my soul found vent in one loud, long and final scream of despair.....

.....God Help My Poor Soul!

The Conqueror Worm

Lo! 'tis a gala night
Within the lonesome latter years!
An angel throng, bewinged, bedight
In veils, and drowned in tears,
Sit in a theatre, to see
A play of hopes and fears,
While the orchestra breathes fitfully
The music of the spheres.

Mimes, in the form of God on high,
Mutter and mumble low,
And hither and thither fly-
Mere puppets they, who come and go
At bidding of vast formless things
That shift the scenery to and fro,
Flapping from out their condor wings
Invisible Wo!

That motley drama - oh, be sure
It shall not be forgot!
With its phantom chased for evermore
By a crowd that seize it not,
Through a circle that ever returneth in
To the self-same spot,

Chapter Sixteen — 'But there was to be no more dallying with the King of Terrors'

And much of Madness, and more of Sin,
And Horror the soul of the plot.
But see, amid the mimic rout
A crawling shape intrude!
A blood-red thing that writhes from out
The scenic solitude!
It writhes! - it writhes! - with mortal pangs
The mimes become its food,
And the seraphs sob at vermin fangs
In human gore imbued.

Out - out are the lights - out all!
And, over each quivering form
The curtain, a funeral pall,
Comes down with the rush of a storm,
And the angels, all pallid and wan,
Uprising, unveiling, affirm
That the play is the tragedy "Man,"
And its hero The Conqueror Worm.

                            EDGAR ALLAN POE

Dedicated to Edgar and Virgina Poe
and Maria Clemm

With grateful acknowledgement to
Edgar Allan Poe